Offerings to the
Muslim Warriors of Malabar

Edited with Commentary and Foreword
by
J.B.P.More

Offerings to the Muslim Warriors of Malabar

Foundation Document of
Colonialism and Clash of Civilisations
(Tr. From the Indo-Arabic work 'Tohfut ul mujahideen')

Edited with Commentary and Foreword
by
J.B.P.More

Saindhavi Publication
2015

Offerings to the Muslim Warriors of Malabar

Foundation Document of Colonialism and Clash of Civilisations
(Tr. From the Indo-Arabic work 'Tohfut ul mujahideen')

First Edition 2015

Edited with Commentary and Foreword
J.B.P. More

Copy right© *J.B.P. More*

Published by
Saindhavi Publications,
359, Secretariat Colony,
Thuraipakkam,
Chennai-600 097.
+91 9442741496

Copies available at
Saindhavi Publications,
359, Secretariat Colony,
Thuraipakkam,
Chennai-600 097.
pradhasaravanan@gmail.com

Pages: 164
Price: ₹ 350/-

ISBN: 978-81-927639-5-8

Printed at
Students Offset Printers, Chennai-600 001.

Contents

Foreword

J.B.P.More

Many historians with a nationalist bent of mind like K.M.Pannikar consider the arrival of the Portuguese in Malabar to be the beginning of the colonial subjugation of India and much of the Eastern world. Some revisionist scholars with a western orientation like Ashin Das Gupta and Sanjay Subrahmanyam do not accept the nationalist historian's stand. Instead they try to minimize the role of Vasco da Gama and the Portuguese in the colonial subjugation of India.[1] At the same time, they ignore or neglect or even deride Sheikh Zainuddin, the foremost historian of Malabar and south India who depicted the Portuguese-Malabar conflict in his sixteenth century work 'Tohfut-ul-mujahideen'.[2]

As early as the eighteenth century, the British scholar Adam Smith had considered the discovery of America by Columbus in 1492 and the discovery of the sea route to India by Vasco da Gama in 1497-98 as the two greatest and most important events in the history of mankind. Many scholars hold that these events changed the course of world history, brought about the meeting of the East and West, broke all barriers of race, culture and language, permitted the spread of new values across the world and contributed to the progress of humanity. For these scholars Vasco da Gama and Columbus and their successors were heroes who braved the oceans and opened up a new chapter in world history, the chapter of European expansion-political, cultural, religious and racial, though they or their successors individually or collectively might have been responsible for many of the ills that were generated by this expansion like slavery, killings, occupation of other peoples lands and colonialism.

In this Introductory Note, I will have to unravel the truth or untruth of at least some of these contentions and determine the nature and significance of the interactions of the Portuguese with the Malabaris and its implications for the future. This will be done on the basis of facts. But before proceeding further, let me first situate the historical context which allowed this interaction to take place.

Historical Context

Islam was born in Arabia in the seventh century. By the eighth century, the conquering Arab/Islamic armies spread in all directions. It reached Sind in north-west India in the east and the Iberian Peninsula in the west. Islam reached north-west India as a conquering force. This expansion brought about racial and cultural intermingling in a large scale. But the southern part of India, especially the Malabar Coast had trade relationship with the Arabs and Persians since a very long time. Thus unlike in northern India, Islam reached the Malabar Coast as well as the East African coast as a peaceful force right from the eighth or ninth centuries. Here too there was racial and cultural intermingling. The great Arab historian al Masudi had mentioned in his work about Muslim settlements on the western coast of India in the ninth century. In the eleventh century, we have the Moroccon traveller Al Idrissi who had referred to Muslim settlements in both Sind and Hind.[3] It is quite obvious from these accounts that Muslim settlements have come into existence on the Malabar Coast between the ninth and eleventh centuries. These settlements seem to have expanded in the following centuries.

According to different versions of a prevailing legend in popular imagination, which seems to have received the backing of some seasoned historians like M.G.S.Narayanan, the last Chera king of Kerala converted to Islam and went to Mecca in the seventh, ninth or twelfth centuries. Before leaving Malabar he is believed to have divided his kingdom between his relatives. Once in Arabia, some credit him to have met Prophet Mohammad himself, while others do not hold this view. While still in Arabia, the king of Kerala passes away. Before he died, it seems that he had instructed some Muslim holy men with a certain Malik Bin Dinar in the lead to go to Kerala and preach Islam. It was thus that Islam came to the Malabar Coast according to this legend.

However, no Arab or Persian traveller to the Malabar Coast and India since the time of Sulaiman al Tajir upto the time of Abder Razak of Persia or Sulaiman al-Mahri of Arabia had left us any account related to the conversion of the Kerala king and the coming to Malabar of Malik bin Dinar and his companions. The Chinese travellers' accounts and the extensive Tamil literature of the period concerned like the Periapuranam, do not mention a word about such a conversion. Even Ibn Batuta who was a keen observer of the events in Malabar had not referred to it.[4] However, this legend seems to have been put down in writing or seems to have suddenly cropped up only after the arrival of the Portuguese in Malabar.

The thirteenth century was a great water-shed in world history. The Mongols invaded Persia and razed Baghdad, the seat of the Abbasid Caliphate to the ground in February 1258. The Caliph himself was executed. The unsuccessful Crusaders wars by which the European powers tried to wrest control of Jerusalem and the Holy Land from the Muslims came to an end in 1272. It was during this period, a Turkish slave dynasty captured power in Delhi and northern India. The Mamluks, another Turkish slave dynasty captured power in Egypt. This coincided with the emergence of Calicut as a major port and centre of spice trade on the Malabar Coast where merchants from the Arab lands, Persia and China, Deccan and Gujarat converged, Spice was carried to the ports of the Mamluk Sultanate and the Persian Gulf from where it was transported overland until it reached Western Europe. The Venetian merchants had entered into commercial treaties with the Mamluks by which they monopolised the spice trade in Europe. The Calicut kingdom was ruled by a Hindu Raja called the Samutiri or the Zamorin. His kingdom was the most powerful and the most prosperous of all the kingdoms of Malabar. Its fame had spread as far as Western Europe.

At the same time at the western extremity of the known world i.e. in Portugal, the Portuguese Christians finally succeeded in pushing the Muslims out of Portugal. They also shook themselves off of Spanish hegemony during the 14th century and emerged as a nation. During the 14th and 15th centuries, it was the turn of the Spaniards to push the Muslims totally out of Iberian Peninsula in the most violent manner. Muslims and Jews were subjected to persecution and forcible conversions to Christianity. This forced many of them to flee to North Africa. The hatred and enmity that the Portuguese and Spaniards had for the Muslims from this period onwards is a fact of history.

In 1453 the Turks conquered Constantinople, the seat of the Byzantine Empire. This was an impossible situation. The Pope and the European monarchs were alarmed. The Pope tried unsuccessfully to push the European powers to restart the Crusader wars. The monarchs of Portugal and Spain realised that they were not in position to take on the Turks and the Arabs who still controlled the land route to India. This naturally pushed them into the ocean to find a sea route to India. Already during the fifteenth century, the Portuguese started to navigate down the western African coast. The Pope became very much enthusiastic about the ventures of Portugal and Spain. Through a series of papal bulls, the Pope assumed the sovereignty of the earth. The papal bull of 1452 granted the King of Portugal the right to attack, conquer, convert or subdue the Muslims, pagans and other unbelievers, to capture their goods and territories, to reduce their persons to perpetual slavery and to transfer their lands and properties to the king of Portugal. The Portuguese thus became the first European nation to indulge in the ignominious slave trade, with the sanction of the Pope. At the same time, Christopher Columbus sponsored by the Spanish king to find a sea route to India stumbled upon America in 1492. He indulged in some of the most heinous crimes against the indigenous peoples of America especially when he was nominated as Governor there. Subsequently the Pope promulgated another Bull by which he divided the non-Christian world between the Portuguese and the Spaniards. The former was to have Brazil and Africa and all lands in the east, while the latter would have the lands in the west, except Brazil. Besides the Pope granted the king of Portugal the right to control all ecclesiastical appointments in all her overseas territories, which became the basis of a State-backed church system.[5]

At this juncture, it is worthwhile to note that the Indian Ocean region, was a region where free trade was the norm, subject to the payment of some duties, as it was the case in Calicut, and where peace prevailed since several centuries, except for the brief period when the Cholas ventured out on the high seas from their base in Tamilnadu. The ships with which the Arabs, Persians, Gujaratis, Chinese and Malabaris traded with foreign countries were made of wood sewn with coir, and the husk of coconut was used to make rot resistant anchors and ropes. They had no artillery on board. As piracy existed to a certain extent on the high seas, some kingdoms like Calicut had developed a navy of their own. The Zamorin of Calicut's navy was manned by the famous Marakkars who acted as a deterrent to put down piracy. Calicut's overseas merchants were also generally made up of Muslims, as the Hindus especially of the higher castes would not take to the sea due to religious scruples.

During the fourteenth and the fifteenth centuries, the Chinese had developed a very powerful navy. Several fleets, consisting of hundreds of ships, huge and small, with several thousand men on board, were sent out of China across the seas to Malabar and beyond to East Africa and the Arab lands. These fleets under a certain Cheng Ho served to show the might and prowess of the Chinese on the ocean rather than anything else. The fleets reached Calicut. But the Chinese in spite of possessing such a huge navy had never intended to colonise any part of Malabar or India. Instead they generally maintained cordial relations with the rulers of Malabar, presented them with costly gifts and never countered or intimidated the Arab, Persian and other Indian traders of the high seas.[6] They never also in their wildest dreams had the intention of imposing their values, ideas and ideologies on any alien land like

Malabar. That was not at all in their agenda. But for reasons we do not know the Chinese retreated from the Indian Ocean region during the second half of the fifteenth century, which left the field clear for other potential sea farers and invaders. In the light of the preceding, it is simply an exaggeration to think or assume like M.N.Pearson that the Chinese would have colonised Europe if they had rounded the Cape and reached Europe. As a matter of fact, there was no necessity for the Chinese or the Arabs or Persians to discover such a route as the land route across the Arab lands was more than practical, economic and profitable, unlike the African sea route.

Vasco da Gama in Malabar

The expedition of Vasco da Gama was a well-planned one which had the full backing of the Portuguese royal establishment and the Roman Catholic Church. The Portuguese seem to have acquired by this period, the formidable Chinese inventions of the compass and gun powder which they put to good use in developing their navigational and warfare techniques and skills. Out of the four ships in which Vasco da Gama and his men travelled in July 1997, three were actually sloops of war, built with iron nails and bolts, with at least twenty guns mounted on them. There were only about 170 men in these ships. Vasco da Gama himself had taken the oath before King Manuel of Portugal that through the voyage, which was a 'Holy Venture', they would proclaim the faith in Lord Jesus Christ, the Son of God and wrest wealth and fame by the force of arms from the hands of the 'barbarians, Moors, pagans and other races.' Armed with the Papal Bulls and the sanction of the royalty, Vasco da Gama and his men set out from Lisbon in a completely religious atmosphere, with the intention to vanquish and conquer. He and his men even confessed before boarding their ships. The Cross of the Order of Christ was painted on the sails of these warships.[7] Thus it is quite obvious that Vasco da Gama's 'holy' expedition to India was never intended to be a peaceful mission. This truth stands confirmed by the fact that wherever the opportunity arose around the African coast as well as in Malabar,

Vasco da Gama and his men never failed to resort to violence, either as a defensive or offensive measure, using the formidable guns and superior arms at their disposal. Even the Hottentots and Bantus were not spared. They were scared away with the firing of gunshots.[8] Besides, the expedition had a strong religious, racial and civilisation dimension. The Portuguese were civilised while the others - non-Europeans were 'barbarians', who needed to be subjected by the force of their arms.

Before proceeding further, I would like to point out that the coming to Malabar of Vasco da Gama and his men by the African sea route at the close of the fifteenth century is not a great navigational exploit from the geographical and historical point of view, as it is generally portrayed to be. In fact, they were forced to take this route as the land route was literally blocked by the Arabs and the Turks. Actually Vasco da Gama had simply followed the route already established by his predecessors like Diogo d'Azambuja and Diogo Cao, who reached the river Zaire and Congo on the western African coast and Bartholomeu Dias who sailed as far as the Cape of Good Hope and Natal in 1487-88. That was the first leg of the journey. The second leg of the journey i.e. the crossing of the Arabian Sea to the Malabar Coast from the East African coast was not Vasco da Gama's discovery at all. Indians, Arabs, and Persians have been criss-crossing the Arabian Sea and the Indian Ocean right from the Persian Gulf to as far as China through the Malacca straits since several hundred years. The discovery of the sea route to China through the Malacca Straits, whoever discovered it was a greater geographical discovery which united the East with the west in various respects and permitted the products of the Far East to reach the western extremity of the known world. Besides, it was not a stupendous task for Vasco da Gama to find someone to guide him across the Arabian Sea to Malabar. In this he seems to have taken the help of the Sultan of Melindi of East Africa.

When Vasco da Gama arrived in India, Malabar was divided into various principalities, of which the most powerful was the King or Zamorin of Calicut. Vasco da Gama and his men had instructions to go to Calicut, the leading port and trade centre on the Malabar Coast. The first man to set foot on Malabar soil was not Vasco da Gama as one would expect. Instead it was a deadly convict by the name of Joao Nunes who was sent by Vasco da Gama on a reconnaissance mission. The Zamorin of Calicut welcomed Vasco da Gama and his men later with open arms in great pomp and splendour and paid the usual courtesies due to a foreign dignitary. But Vasco da Gama suspicious and over-cautious right from the beginning very soon ended up committing a diplomatic blunder of the first order when he gave the king who was used to receiving costly gifts like gold and silk from foreign dignitaries like the Chinese Cheng Ho and the Persian ambassador Abd-er-Razak, some cheap gifts consisting of hats, hoods, striped cloth, some sugar, oil and honey, which could be had from the local market itself. The Zamorin as well as his principal merchants who were Muslims were highly displeased with the condescending attitude of Vasco Da Gama. Besides, Vasco da Gama would not allow a Muslim to read the Arabic message of King Manuel to the Zamorin. All this only showed that the general hatred and enmity that the Portuguese had for the Muslims in their homelands had been carried on as far as Malabar by Vasco da Gama and his men. Besides, the latter chose to reside not in the Muslim or Hindu or even in the Christian quarters of Calicut city, but in an abandoned Chinese quarter, in spite of the fact that he and his men were supposed to have believed that the Zamorin and his subjects (as well as many eastern kings) were Christians. There is also no instance of Vasco da Gama celebrating any mass with them in the Malabar soil, unlike on the African coast. In spite of Vasco da Gama's blunders, the Zamorin allowed Vasco da Gama to set up a warehouse for his goods. But Vasco da Gama would not pay the duties that were customary to be paid in Calicut. He ended up taking some 18 Malabaris as hostages in order secure his merchandise stored in the warehouse.[9]

Right from the start Vasco da Gama realised the influence

wielded by the Muslim merchants in Malabar. This was not at all conducive to Portuguese trade interests and their desire to propagate Christianity. Vasco da Gama even tried to wean the Zamorin away from the Muslims during his short stay. Finally he left Calicut with sufficient Malabar spices which procured immense profits back home. On his return to Portugal, Vasco da Gama relayed all information concerning Malabar to the Portuguese king. The Roman Catholic Church too became aware of the obstacles posed by the Muslims to the expansion of Christianity in Malabar. We know the consequences that followed, which had been fairly well documented. King Manuel styled himself thenceforth as the 'Lord of the Conquest, the Navigation and the Commerce in Ethiopia, Arabia, Persia and India'.[10]

The Portuguese king sent fleet after fleet into the Indian Ocean and to Malabar. It started in 1500 with Pedro Alvarez Cabral's fleet of thirteen powerfully armed ships, with the latest canons made of bronze. In 1502, Vasco da Gama himself came back to the Malabar Coast with 20 armed ships and a thousand men. There is ample recorded evidence to prove that he following Cabral inaugurated an era of large-scale violence, massacres and looting in the Indian Ocean and Malabar.[11] This situation continued almost all throughout the sixteenth century. Thus the Indian Ocean which was a zone of free trade and peace since several centuries, became an arena of conflict and tension, within a few years after the Portuguese reached Malabar by the Oceanic route. This had a telling effect on the political and economic power of the Zamorin and the Muslim merchants. It undermined Malabar and Muslim trade irreversibly.

In 1507-8 Socotra in the Gulf of Aden and Hormuz in the Persian Gulf fell into Portuguese hands. In 1510, Admiral Afonso da Albuquerque defeated the troops of Sultan of Bijapur and captured Goa which became the headquarters of the Portuguese in India and Asia, with a Viceroy appointed by the King of Portugal. The State-backed church system also came into vogue in Goa. In 1511, the Portuguese captured Malacca.

It should not be forgotten that during the sixteenth century Portugal was a small nation with about one million or more people, out of which only a few thousands were operating in the Indian Ocean region and on the Malabar Coast. They did not have the numbers and material means to invade and acquire more territories in the interior of Malabar or the Deccan or northern India against the military might of the Sultan of Bijapur and the Mughals or to permanently dominate the vast expanse of the Indian Ocean waters. But they had sufficient means to hold on to their coastal forts and territories. Besides with superior arms and ships at their disposal, they exercised a certain dominance of the high seas, which was enough to bring down Muslim trade in the Indian Ocean region, in which Malabar and its Muslims were key players. As far as Malabar is concerned they built formidable forts at various vantage points by befriending some local Malabar rulers like the kings of Cochin, Quilon and Cannanore who were against the predominance of the Zamorin of Calicut. The Portuguese actually utilised local rivalries to their advantage, especially to counter the power of the Zamorin and his Muslim allies. Thus the Portuguese were the early practitioners of the policy of 'divide and rule' in Malabar and India in order to establish themselves on a sound basis on the Malabar Coast. They also took to sparing those Malabar rulers and others like the merchants who would side with them or were submissive to them like the Raja of Cochin and smashing the rebels like the Zamorin of Calicut and the Muslim merchant Mamalli Marakkar of Kannur who would never submit to them and their dictates.

In order to offset their numerical disadvantage, it was also the policy of the Portuguese to resort to 'calculated racial cross-breeding or 'deliberate miscegenation' all along the African and Indian coasts and create Christian populations of mixed descent, who were expected to be loyal to the Portuguese, Christian and Western values.[12] All this heralded the colonial subjugation of India and much of the eastern world. The Roman Catholic Church and the Portuguese royal establishment were the prime inspirers, instigators and initiators of this subjugation. Men like Vasco da Gama were tools in their hands. Unlike the Chinese, the Portuguese had a different agenda, which involved not just colonisation of other people's lands by the force of their arms, but also impose their values, ideologies, religion and civilisation upon others in the course of time, without ever snapping their ties with their original homelands from where they were remote-controlled.

The violence unleashed by the Portuguese had no parallel in the Indian Ocean waters and coasts. Vasco da Gama himself had personally indulged in some of the most heinous violence and atrocities especially against the Muslims. On 1st October 1502 he mercilessly ordered the killing of 700 innocent Muslim pilgrims who were returning from Mecca to Malabar, which included women and children, by setting their ship on fire with gun powder, after looting them. On 27 October 1502, he seized 50 Malabaris at sea, as the Zamorin would not banish the Muslims from Calicut as demanded by him, got their heads, legs and hands cut off and sent ashore in a boat with a message in Arabic asking the Zamorin 'to make curry out of the severed limbs'. Not satisfied with this, he bombarded Calicut from the sea for three consecutive days and razed it to the ground, probably killing several hundred people in the process. Later, in January 1525, a year after Vasco da Gama came back as Viceroy of Portuguese possessions in India, the Portuguese confronted Mamalli Marakkar, one of the richest Malabar merchant, based in Cannanore. They caught him, cut his hands off and hanged him on the wall of the Portuguese fort of Cannanore, to strike terror in the hearts of the Muslims and the local rulers. Vasco da Gama and his successors were guilty of various other atrocities and heinous crimes off the Malabar Coast.[13] In the light of these facts, Vasco da Gama can be rightly deemed as the inaugurator of the gun-boat trade and politics in the Indian Ocean region. He and his successors used unbridled violence to terrorise the Zamorin and the Muslims and make them bend to their wishes. Vasco da Gama's heinous crimes in Malabar and the Indian Ocean were clearly a case of crime against humanity. The Portuguese royal establishment and the Roman Catholic church, which always had the hegemonic mission of converting the whole world to Christianity, need to bear responsibility for these crimes, for it was they who had sponsored Vasco Da Gama and his men to find the sea route to India and had given them the necessary sanctions to act in a violent manner against the unbelievers, Moors, pagans, barbarians and other races.

Since Cabral's time, the policy of the Portuguese tended to monopolise the spice trade in the region. They introduced the art of economic blockade in a free trade zone. They even expected Indian and Malabar ships to pay and procure cartazes or passes from them to ply or trade on the high seas. They forced all ships to call at their ports on the Malabar Coast and pay customs duties to them. Through such methods they generated considerable revenue to the great detriment of the rulers of the Malabar Coast. This was unprecedented in Indian and Malabar history. Apart from tending to monopolise trade in the region, the Portuguese also had the mission to propagate Christianity, which was a central part of European civilisation. This they did to the best of their ability. Missionaries were deployed all along the Malabar Coast. There are records of them having indulged in forcible conversions of Muslims and Hindus to Christianity. They also desecrated and even destroyed mosques and temples whenever the opportunity arose. Stephen Dale had pointed out in his work the desire of the Portuguese to extirpate and disrupt Islamic communities on the Malabar Coast. They also were responsible for implementing the notorious Inquisition all along the coast. The Inquisition practised here was one of most cruel in entire Christendom. Voltaire was flabbergasted by it. The Syrian Christians of Malabar, who were Christians even before Portuguese arrival in Malabar bore the brunt of it. They were specially coerced and forced to submit themselves to the authority of the Pope.[14]

A Review of Tohfut-ul-mujahideen

Sheikh Zainuddin, a learned man of Malabar, whose father was the Imam of the famous Ponnani mosque, was terribly shaken by all the violence and injustice unleashed by the Portuguese on the Malabar Coast, which decimated his compatriots. He wrote a whole book in the latter part of the sixteenth century describing this violence in all its details and the general conflict between the Portuguese and the Zamorin and his Muslim allies all throughout the sixteenth century. The title of the book was Tohfut-ul-mujahideen, which means 'Offerings to the Muslim Warriors of Malabar'. This pioneering historical work remained in obscurity until the British conquered India.

Actually in the year 1757, the British won a significant victory against the Muslim power in Bengal at the Battle of Plassey. This victory signalled the entry of the British as a dominant ruling power in northern India. During this period, Persian was the official language of the Mughal Empire and most of its successor states. So knowledge of Persian became a natural necessity for the British in India. They retained it as the official language. They started learning and mastering the Persian language as it was still the prime language of communication in political India. It is not surprising to note that the early French Indologist, Anquetil Duperron took a particular interest in Persian and all that was related to it during his travels in India in the 1750s. It is also not surprising to note that the British administrators and scholars too devoted a great attention to Persian. It all seems to have started with the publication of the 'Grammar of the Persian Language' in London in 1771 by Sir William Jones. He had studied Persian and Arabic at Oxford, before he was employed in Calcutta.

In southern India too, Persian was the official language of the Hyderabad Nizams and the Nawabs of Carnatic. With the defeat of Tipu Sultan in 1799, the British had become the dominant political power in south India. The Nawab of Carnatic had been rendered powerless and dependent upon the British. But as these rulers had Persian as their official language, the British too followed their footsteps in Madras. They needed men who knew Persian and also Arabic, the sacred language of the Muslims. When the College of Fort St.George was established in 1812, they needed men to teach Persian and Arabic. They also needed men to write books in Persian and Arabic for the use of the students in the Fort

St. George College and the schools and for the purpose of teaching. It was thus that an army officer, well-versed in Persian and Arabic, called Lieutenant M.J.Rowlandson, was recruited in the 1820s to be the Acting Secretary to the Board for the College of Fort St.George and for Public Instruction. Very soon, he was made Secretary. He was actually the Persian interpreter of the army headquarters of Fort St.George.

In 1828, he published a book called 'An Analysis of Arabic Quotations which occur in Gulistan' of Muslih-ud-Deen Sheikh Sadi. In this book, he added certain 'Remarks on Arabic Grammar', both in English and Persian languages. This was actually extracted from the *'Munit'khib Alsurf'* by Moulavi Syed Ameer Hyder. This book was actually written for the use of the College of Fort St.George. This book no doubt demonstrated his mastery of both the Persian and Arabic languages.

Later in 1833, he brought out a book on the 'Rudiments of Natural Philosophy'. This book was at the same time a compilation and translation by him, expressly produced for the use of the Persian class in the college of Fort St.George and other schools of the Madras Presidency or province. In the same year, he brought out a translation of the *Tohfut ul-mujahideen* of Sheikh Zainuddin of Malabar, the sixteenth century south Indian Arabic work. The translation of this work of the Sheikh of Malabar, with instructive comments and notes by M.J.Rowlandson is a must for every historian working on Keralam, south Indian and Indian maritime history. He rendered the Arabic *Tohfut-ul-mujahideen* as 'Offerings to the Warriors of Malabar' in English. But for M.J.Rowlandson, the Sheikh's work would have probably remained in oblivion for some more time.

Sheikh Zainuddin lived in the latter part of the sixteenth century in Malabar. He seems to be a descendant of Arab migrants to Ma'bar, as he bears the title of al-Ma'bari. It is quite possible that he was of mixed Indo-Arab parentage. Generally, the southern Tamil coast or country was known as Ma'bar in Arabic. In the present state of our knowledge we do not know when his ancestors had migrated to Ma'bar. The Sheikh himself had not told us anything about it or about his ancestry in his work.

It seems that the Sheikh's ancestor, Zainuddin al-Ma'bari al-Malibari (d.1522) lived in Bijapur for a long time. Bijapur was then ruled by the Adil Shahis. They were mostly Shias of Persian origin, who looked to the Shah of Iran for allegiance and spiritual leadership. Al-Malibari was a versatile scholar who wrote extensively on subjects ranging from the hadith and the fiqh to Islamic mysticism and Arabic poetry. His Sufi poem *Hidayat al-adhkya ila Tariqat il Auliya* 'Guidance of the Intelligent' was well known. His son, Abdul Aziz added a commentary to it called *Maslak ul Adhkya*. It is believed that Al-Malibari was the first *makhdum* of the Ponnani religious centre, established in the fifteenth century in Malabar.

It is quite unfortunate and astonishing that some scholars like Sanjay Subrahmanyam and Stephen Dale had preferred to ignore M.J.Rowlandson's translation of the Sheikh's work. Instead, they seem to have relied on David Lopez's translation of the work into Portuguese. Thus they missed the useful historical comments of Rowlandson. Sanjay Subrahmanyam, basing himself on the work of Lopez, goes to the extent of dismissing Sheikh Zainuddin as a disgruntled fanatic and jihadist, without taking into account the extraordinarily difficult situation in which the Zamorin of Malabar and his Muslim subjects found themselves due to Portuguese intrusion into the Indian Ocean region and Malabar and the systematic oppression of the Muslims and their religion and the destruction of their trade. The Sheikh was so exasperated by the atrocities committed by the Portuguese against the Zamorin of Calicut and his Nair soldiers and the Marakkars who manned his navy, for about a century that he had no other alternative except to call the Muslims to stand up and fight. He of course formulated his call in the form of jihad. His jihad was directed against the Portuguese and never against any local king.[15]

Besides, the Sheikh accused the Portuguese 'infidels' of great moral depravity and irreligiousness, indulging in things contrary to the Christian values and religion. This stands confirmed later by the accounts of the French Jesuit priests who came to India during the seventeenth and eighteenth centuries.[16] But the Sheikh knew that he was making a last-ditch attempt to retrieve Muslim fortunes in Malabar which had been heavily obliterated by the Portuguese. He knew that his call was not going to be successful.

M.J.Rowlandson did not go about beating the bush or indulge in hair-splitting arguments like some of the modern scholars to ascertain if the Portuguese had indulged in violence and atrocities on the Malabar Coast. Instead, he relied on facts, the facts that he had gathered from the works of European chroniclers and writers. He compared them with the Sheikh's work and came to the conclusion that the accounts related in the Sheikh's work was very much identical to the accounts of the European and Portuguese chroniclers of the sixteenth century. He also concluded on the basis of these accounts, both European and that of the Sheikh that the Portuguese were indeed guilty of terrible acts of barbarity from the time they set foot in Malabar. The principal victims were of course the Muslims of Malabar. Many other historians European and western historians had acknowledged this fact.[17]

Sheikh Zainuddin, was the grandson of Zainuddin al-Ma'bari al-Malibari and son of Abdul Aziz, who was Qazi. The Sheikh's *Tohfut-ul-mujahideen* is a unique work of the sixteenth century of great historical importance for peninsular India and the Indian Ocean region. It is the first of its kind at least as far as southern India is concerned, if we do not take into account the *Musakavamsakavya* (Poem on the genealogy of the Musaka dynasty of Elimala of northern Kerala) of the eleventh century by Atula, which contains some historical matter.[18]

The Sheikh was not a court historian or chronicler as we find in the Mughal courts and the other sultanates of the Deccan or northern India. Instead his work was an individual attempt to retrace the history of Malabar and its Muslims particularly. It was also an attempt to describe the geography, geo-politics, social and economic conditions and the cultural and religious factors of Malabar. That he did all this extremely well and coherently with a high sense of historical consciousness, within the restricted space of his small work is itself something remarkable in the development of modern historical writing in south India. As far as Keralam and south India is concerned the Sheikh is no doubt a precursor of modern historical writing. So it will not be wrong to conclude that historical consciousness was present in south India even before the Europeans colonised India.

The Sheikh's ancestors had not come to India as conquerors. They came as merchants or sailors or religious men. Besides, the areas of Ma'bar and Malabar, in which the Sheikh operated was not under Muslim rule, unlike the Deccan and northern India. The Sheikh dedicated his work to Sultan Ali Adil Shah of Bijapur, one of the great ruling sovereigns of southern India. He did this probably because he was acquainted with the Bijapur sultanate since his grandfather's time. However the Sultan of Bijapur who happened to be a Sunni at that time was never known to be the patron of his work. The work is a standing testimony for not only his mastery of the Arabic language, but also his deep knowledge of the Koran and the Islamic religion, traditions and customs. M.J.Rowlandson, the accomplished British scholar in Arabic and Persian had amply attested this fact.[19]

Anyone going through the work of the Sheikh would easily understand that he was a deeply religious and truthful person in the Islamic sense of the terms. There was no reason for him to lie on anything. Whatever information that he had recorded in his work, he would have obtained from various books and mosque records, through interviews, his own observations and experiences and other oral sources. This does not mean that there could be no mistakes in his recordings, for he might have sometimes noted down even wrong information, especially with regard to the origin and early history of the Muslims of Malabar, on the basis of some floating legends. He might also have made some wrong observations. It should be noted that the Sheikh himself had remarked in his work that the Portuguese had made it a point to destroy all the books and archives in the mosques of Malabar. Though this is possible, yet there are no corroborating evidences to attest this contention. There is also no evidence that the Sheikh drew his subject-matter from earlier literature, for he had not told us anything about it.

It is however significant to note that the Sheikh in his work does not endorse the popular belief that the Kerala king, Cheraman Perumal went to Mecca, met the Prophet and converted to Islam during the lifetime of the Prophet itself. Instead, he seems to maintain that the conversion of Cheraman Perumal took place in the ninth century and Muslim messengers came to Malabar to spread Islam during this period. However, he never cites the source of his information. He never refers to Hadith or any Islamic literature to buttress his contention. Instead he seems to have based his account on floating legends several centuries after the supposed conversion actually took place. The claim in some quarters that the Cheraman Perumal actually met the Prophet and converted to Islam has no adequate evidence in the Hadith literature. Sheikh Zainuddin, being an Islamic scholar, would have mentioned about it if it had been so. There is no reference in the Hadith to any Malabar king by the name of Cheraman Perumal meeting the Prophet. But there seems to be a possibility that some chiefs from the Sind region might have met the Prophet. Some scholars claim that there is a reference to it in the Hadith. However, as the Hadith literature itself is subject to various extrapolations, it is highly difficult to determine the spurious from the genuine.

The Sheikh seems to be a widely travelled man. He was well aware of Muslim power in the Middle-east, in Egypt, Turkey, Persia, Gujarat, northern India and the Deccan. However, he seems to be not aware of Muslim or Moorish power in north-western Maghreb and southern and Eastern Europe, particularly in Spain and Portugal. His knowledge of the geography of India and the Arabian Sea region is quite impressive. He knew a lot about the social, economic and political situation of Malabar. His knowledge of the traditions and customs of the Malabar society in which he lived and evolved and the situation of the Muslims in that society is equally impressive.

According to the Sheikh, generally the Muslims in Malabar did not face any opposition in the largely non-Muslim Malabar society, except on rare occasions. They were allowed by the Hindu kings to live their lives as Muslims, according to their own jurisdiction and follow their traditions and customs in full freedom, without infringing the customary laws of the land, by which relationship between Muslims and non-Muslims were regulated. Besides, the Malabar rulers like the Zamorin of Calicut were favourably disposed towards the Muslims and never prevented conversions to Islam. All Muslims even converts from the lower castes were treated on an equal footing by the rest of the population. In fact, the Muslims welcomed these conversions and even spent money to accommodate the new converts in Islam. It is quite probable that some members of the lower castes converted to Islam because of a certain equality prevailing in the Malabar Muslim society and in order to escape from the hereditary caste disabilities. In any case, the Sheikh was fully aware that the rigid Hindu social order based on a hierarchical set-up of society, where the lower castes were at the receiving end, favoured very much the conversion of the members of these castes to Islam. As a matter of fact, the egalitarian ideology of Islam posed a challenge to the Hindu hereditary caste system, of which the Hindu kings and the higher castes seem to have been hardly aware during this period.

The Sheikh never found it inconvenient for the Muslims in Malabar who constituted about one-tenth of the population during his time to be the subjects of a benevolent non-Muslim Hindu sovereign like the Zamorin. This becomes obvious when one goes through his work, *Tohfut-ul-mujahideen*. On the whole, a definite social harmony prevailed between the Muslims and the non-Muslims, arbitrated by the Zamorin. There is not the slightest indication that the Sheikh desired to establish an Islamic state in Malabar, by overthrowing the Zamorin or any other local Hindu sovereign. He was actually extremely loyal to the Zamorin and looked upon the Nair soldiers and the Marakkars who fought the Portuguese as warriors defending the interests of the Zamorin and his kingdom.

The Portuguese factor, Duarte Barbosa, who lived in Kannur in the beginning of the sixteenth century had noted in his work that but for the arrival of the Portuguese, the whole Malabar Coast would have become Muslim very soon. Barbosa was probably right to some extent, because the Sheikh had noted the conversions that were taking place to Islam during the sixteenth century from the local religions, in spite of Portuguese arrival. Today, after nearly five centuries, the Muslim population accounts for about one-fourth of the total population of Kerala, concentrated mainly in northern Kerala, where in some areas they are even a majority. Many of them especially in the interior areas seem to have been drawn from the lower Hindu castes.

Surprisingly the Sheikh had never chosen in his work to use the word 'Hindu' to describe the non-Muslims of Malabar, most certainly because the word had not come into usage during the sixteenth century in Malabar. The term 'Hinduism' as well as the terms 'India' or 'Indian' was actually European inventions, which were unquestioningly adopted by the Indians. It is noteworthy that while all countries bordering India had chosen to revert to their ancient names or indigenous names, India alone retains still the name attributed to it by the colonialists. When the Mughals and Arabs called India as Hindustan (the land of the Hindus) and Al Hind or Hind respectively, it never really had a religious or colonial connotation. Instead it possessed a geographical and ethnic significance. Both Muslims and non-Muslims were considered as belonging to Hindustan and Hind by them. The Arabic term 'Hindi' would signify 'One who hails from Hind'. Of course the term 'Hindu' itself owes its origin to the Arabic Hind or Hindi and the Persian Hindustan. Even today, Arabs call India as Hind. But things as we know changed during the colonial period, when the Europeans attributed a restrictive meaning to the term 'Hindu' to signify only those Indians who subscribed to the indigenous religions of India. Following this logics, they even replaced the Mughal term Hindustan by the European term India to signify the entire sub-continent.

However, the Sheikh was well aware of the peculiar customs and traditions of the non-Muslims of Malabar or 'infidels' as he would call them. He has described to some extent the social system of the land, based on caste and caste hierarchy. The Namboodiri Brahmin was placed at the top of this hierarchy, followed by the martial Nairs. The Tiyyas, who were agriculturists, were placed below the Nairs. The carpenters, the ironsmiths, the fishermen came after the Tiyyas, while below these castes there were several other inferior castes who worked in the farms and agricultural lands.

It is noteworthy that the Sheikh had mentioned in his work about the continuance of some non-Muslim customs like the *marumakkattayam* or matriarchal custom among the coastal Muslims of northern Malabar like Kannur and its adjoining regions, where inheritance rights of property and political power does not go to the immediate offspring, but to the nieces and nephews. This demonstrates that these Muslims were of definite high caste Nair extraction, while the other Muslims, who followed patriarchy, were in all probability mostly of a lower caste extraction or Brahmins. The patriarchal system prevailed among the other castes like the Brahmins, fishermen, labourers, painters and carpenters and other similar castes where the immediate offspring inherited the property of the deceased parents.

The Sheikh mentions about some customary laws which restricted social relationship between the various castes, especially between the men and women of the various castes. Any transgression of these laws was punishable. Sometimes the transgressors were thrown out of the caste. If for example a Nair man had sexual relationship with a lower caste woman, he became an outcaste. In this case, the transgressor had no other alternative but to convert to Islam or Christianity. This was no doubt advantageous to the latter religions to increase their numbers. It must not be forgotten that the Sheikh was viewing Malabar society from the Islamic point of view.

However the Sheikh does not tell us anything more about the legendary persecution of the lower castes by the higher castes, which after all might not have been so acute as to merit attention during the sixteenth century, at least in Malabar, but which might have aggravated subsequently with the arrival of Europeans, who introduced the notion of private landownership, with which they were accustomed in their homelands. It is this notion that had brought about the division between landowners and agricultural serfs, slaves or labourers. It is noteworthy at this juncture that the Sheikh had expressly stated in his work that the cultivators and tiller never paid any tax to the chiefs or rulers who were nominal trustees of the land. In other words, there were no landownership rights and therefore no payment of land and harvest tax to the chiefs. In fact, the idea of private landownership itself, as the Europeans understood it, never seem to have existed in Malabar. It was only with the subsequent introduction of landownership rights by the Europeans that the various castes and communities appear to get more and more estranged from one another, with the resultant injustices and inequalities. All this resulted in peasant revolts, pitting landless labourers against the landowners and the State, especially during British colonial rule in Malabar that started with the defeat of Tipu Sultan in 1792 at the hands of the English. These revolts especially in the southern parts of Malabar were repressed in the most ruthless manner by the British, in which many peasant rebels, who were converts or descendants of converts to Islam, lost their lives. If there had been such revolts during the sixteenth century or before, the Sheikh would have definitely noted it in his work.

As a matter of fact, there were no such revolts reported by Sheikh Zainuddin during this period, as the idea of private landownership or property had not yet affected the Malabar mind, society and societal relationships during the Sheikh's lifetime. But with the arrival of the Europeans, especially the British this idea spread like a virus in Malabar. It took a heavy toll not just in Malabar, but also in many other parts of south Asia and the world, in its various avatars. Feudalism, capitalism and now globalisation (global capitalism) has proliferated upon this viral idea. It has led to innumerable and unending conflicts, wars, massacres, tensions, injustices and inequalities in society and human relationships. But still for reasons that are beyond the scope of this book, man has been forced or persuaded to get accustomed to live with this virus even today, assuming that it is the most rational and progressive thing to do. It is simply an illusion and gross irrationality to think that human beings will become equal through private property.

Moreover, the Sheikh does not fail to point out in his work the licentiousness that existed customarily among the Nair women, who usually had two, three or even more husbands. Besides, only the elder son of a Namboodiri family had the right to marry while the others had Nair concubines. He also points out that the Nairs especially expose the upper part of their bodies, while Nair women deck themselves during festival times so that their bodily beauty is visually enjoyed by all men. It must not be forgotten that the Sheikh was a Muslim and in Muslim society, women covered their bodies with clothes so that men do not cast their lustful eyes on them and they do not become the objects of men's promiscuous sexual desires. This was part of their notion of civilisation and progress. Therefore it is not surprising to note that the Sheikh dismisses many of these indigenous social customs as unreasonable and without meaning. He was of course viewing all this from an Islamic point of view. The Sheikh does not adopt a very harsh tone towards these customs. Instead he asserts that it was due to such customs also that many were attracted by Islam and converted. The Sheikh, who is buried at Chombala, near Mahé within the precincts of the Kunhipalli mosque, about seventy kilometres north of Calicut, would definitely be turning in his grave if he realises that in today's Hind, many women dare to bare themselves, in the name of fashion, cinema, culture, business, profession, aesthetics, modernity, progress and liberty, so that all men and women of all ages may have the possibility of enjoying them visually and have a sexual feeling and attitude towards them.[20]

M.J.Rowlandson was a deeply religious and largely straight forward scholar. He was not just interested in translating the Sheikh Zainuddin's work into English. Instead, he also commented upon various historical and religious aspects found in Sheikh Zainuddin's work. He compared them with the Islamic religious texts and also the works of Portuguese and other western chroniclers and historians, in which he was well-versed. That is why his translation of Sheikh Zainuddin's work and his extensive comments upon it, stands out as one of the most noteworthy works, among the many translations of Indian literature into English done by the Europeans during the late eighteenth century and the nineteenth century.

M.J.Rowlandson was well-versed in several languages including Arabic, Latin and Portuguese. He had a deep knowledge of the history of Islam and the Islamic theology, law and jurisprudence. He was aware of the works and commentaries on the Koran and the Hadiths of the Islamic scholars like Jellaludeen, al-Beidawi and Abulfeda. He also did not fail to compare wherever necessary the Sheikh's work, with the accounts of the Muslim chroniclers of India like Mahomed Kasim Ferishta. Besides, he was well-versed with Muslim or rather Mughal history in India, as well as the origin and evolution of the Jews and Syrian Christians or Nestorians in Malabar and their interaction with the Portuguese. He also had at his disposal considerable knowledge of the local Malabar society through the works of European scholars like Fra Paolino Bartolomeo and Francis Buchanan. Rowlandson had pointed out on several occasions in his study of Portuguese high-handedness and intolerance, not only towards the Muslims, but also towards the Syrian Christians, who were literally forced to join the Roman Catholic religion and were also subjected to Inquisition.

Rowlandson's translation stuck very closely to the Arabic original of the Sheikh, unlike the translation of Muhammad Husayn Nainar, which was rendered in a very prosaic form more than one century later and published in 1942. The commentaries and notes by Rowlandson, appended to his translation make his work really remarkable and useful to the understanding of not only the work of the Sheikh, but also various other historical factors related to the history of southern India. One could admit without exaggeration that his was a pioneering work of comparative history of a very high order.

The Frenchman Pyrard de Laval who was also on the Malabar Coast had also given us a graphic account of the atrocities to which the Muslims were subjected by the Portuguese in the latter part of the sixteenth century, when the Portuguese had finally succeeded in weaning the Zamorin away from the Muslims. The Marakkar chief, Kunhali Marakkar IV along with forty of his companions were beheaded in Goa, on a scaffold raised in the large square in front of the Portuguese Viceregal Palace. After the beheading of the Marakkar chief, his body was quartered and exhibited on the Goa beach and his head salted and sent to Cannanore, where it was to be stuck on a standard to terrorise the Moors. But before the execution, the Fathers of the various orders tried to convert the Marakkar chief to Christianity. Besides, scholars and specialists of the expansion of Christianity like D'Sa and KS.Latourette and other scholars like C.R.Boxer and Stephen Dale have documented in their works many details of Portuguese atrocities on the Malabar Coast and how the Portuguese smashed the rebels and spared the slaves. In one instance 12000 Muslims were forcibly converted to Christianity at Quilon. K.S.Latourette concluded that the Portuguese were 'guilty of unspeakable acts of cruelty and barbarism'.

The Sheikh himself had lamented that the various rulers of Malabar, of the Deccan and northern India were disunited and quarrelling with one another, while the Portuguese were united under one banner, receiving orders for what they should do in India from far away Portugal.. Consequently he knew that the chances of winning the war against the Portuguese were minimal. However, it is clear from the preceding that the Sheikh was among the earliest Indian stalwarts and historians who viewed al-Hind as one geographical unit, though its rulers vied with one another. He was to my knowledge the first Indian writer and learned man to recognise the serious disunity prevailing among the Indian rulers during the sixteenth century, which he feared would pave the way for the Portuguese to maintain their territorial foothold in India, and participate and take sides in the quarrels between the local Indian rulers, often playing one against the other and establishing their hegemony durably. The other Europeans who came to India after the Portuguese simply followed the footsteps of the Portuguese in their dealings with Indians and colonised the whole Indian sub-continent by the end of the eighteenth century.

In fact, heeding to the call of the Sheikh, nobody came to the rescue of the Malabar Muslims and the Zamorin. There was no response from the Bijapur and other sultanates of the Deccan, the Mughal emperor and the Sultans of Gujarat, who were all parts of al-Hind. Even in Malabar, the Hindu kings of Kannur, Cochin and Quilon, not to speak of other smaller kings, ever lift their finger in favour of the Nairs and Muslims of Malabar or the Zamorin, who relentlessly defied the Portuguese colonisers. To the Marakkars and the Zamorin goes the credit of resisting first the colonisation of Malabar and Hind and the subsequent imposition of a globalised colonial economy of the capitalistic and machine-based type. Capitalism was not the invention of the Malabaris. The merchants of Malabar had never attempted to control the means of production, the production process and the produce like the capitalists of the west. The Sheikh knew that the Zamorin of Calicut despite being a Hindu was the only king who sponsored the fight of the Marakkars against the Portuguese. In fact, the Marakkars fought the Portuguese on behalf of the Zamorin as they were Zamorin's subjects and were part and parcel of the defence machinery of the Zamorin.

Conclusions and Observations

In the light of what I have exposed above, especially with regard to the atrocities perpetrated by the Portuguese in the Indian Ocean Region and Malabar, it becomes highly impossible to support the contentions of revisionist scholars like Ashin Das Gupta that the Portuguese did not change anything in the Indian Ocean region, that they had come to the region with the most peaceful of intentions, that the conflict between the Malabaris and Portuguese had no religious colouring and that the Portuguese were in partnership with Indians all throughout the sixteenth century. Besides they hold that if they had not come India would be plunged in ignorance and slavery.[21]

It is also not right to minimize the atrocities committed by the Portuguese on the Malabar Coast by insinuating that Indians were used to violence and brutality even before the arrival of the Portuguese. Ashin Das Gupta had insinuated that in terms of time the Mughals, who had come to India later than Vasco da Gama, had subjected India even before the Europeans and therefore it is not right to hold Vasco da Gama as the originator of the colonial subjugation of India. Sanjay Subrahmanyam has become the latest proponent of such revisionist views and theories that tended to decriminalise the role of Vasco da Gama and by implication the Portuguese king and the Roman Catholic Church in the colonial subjugation of India.

But what the revisionist historians seem to have forgotten is the fact that even before the arrival of Vasco da Gama, India had been invaded by the Turks and Afghans and before the Turks, by many others. But these people as well as the Mughals who had come to India as invaders, had made India their home and they never received orders from the rulers of their original homelands of what they have to do in India and how. But this was not the case with Vasco da Gama and his successors and the other Europeans who followed them. They never let themselves to be Indianised as it was the case with the Mughals. Actually, it was the Mughals who had made India their only home, and who called India as 'Hindustan'. They never took away the riches of India to their homelands, for they had made 'Hindustan' as their homeland. That is why we cannot talk of the colonial subjugation of India by the Mughals and we can talk of the colonial subjugation of India by the Europeans, bearing in mind that this form of subjugation is an improved version of slavery, whatever good that such slavery might have engendered. This subjugation was not just physical. It also involved the imposition of various aspects of the civilisation, culture, values and ideologies of the coloniser on those of the colonised including capitalism, which survived even after the departure of the colonisers.[22]

Besides, scholars should also think about the atrocities perpetrated by the Portuguese and the Spaniards in America and Africa due to the discovery of the Red Indian continent by Columbus in 1492, under the same papal and royal impulse, when they try to minimize the role of Vasco da Gama in the subjugation of Asia and India. Millions of Africans were transported as slaves across the Atlantic to America. Many thousands or millions died on account of this. The lands of the Red Indians were occupied and all sorts of atrocities were committed against them. It is not right on the part of scholars to gloss over these atrocities, which are irrefutable historical facts and not some mechanistic forms of comparative history or cultural exoticism, as Sanjay Subrahmanyam would want us to believe. They were the outcome of Vasco da Gama coming to India and Columbus discovering America. In the face of these facts, it is completely out of step on the part of Subrahmanyam to lecture the scholarly audiences about "connected histories", when it is clear as crystal that the history of colonisation and European expansion in the world had all the trappings of "confrontational history", which inaugurated a new era of clash of civilisations.[23]

Moreover the colonisation of America and the intrusion of the Portuguese into the Indian Ocean and Malabar at the expense of the indigenous races and peoples had happened much before the industrial revolution actually saw the light in Europe during the second half of the eighteenth century. Therefore it is impossible to accept the arguments put forward by some scholars like M.N.Pearson that industrial development and the technological capacity it gave the Europeans led to colonisation and subjugation of the world and that this would have happened even if the Portuguese had not rounded the Cape in 1498 seems to be rather weak and fallacious.

This confrontational culture and clash of civilizations even gained a certain dubious scientific and philosophical legitimacy in the year 1859, with the publication of Charles Darwin's highly controversial speculative theory of evolution related to the origin of life and the human species from some primordial chemical soup through a struggle for existence and the survival of the fittest. Darwin seems to have even thought that the 'civilised' Europeans were the fittest of all to survive and the 'uncivilised' and 'savage' races were bound to vanish in the struggle for life probably in some strange contrived post-modern chemical 'melting pot'. Some thought that slavery and colonialism that started with the Portuguese were parts of this struggle and therefore justified. Many European philosophers, anthropologists and ethnologists found Darwin's assertions as scientific and more or less followed Darwin's way of thinking and philosophy. If we follow Darwin's logics, European civilisation and values, which are considered as modern, has to triumph ultimately at the expense of all other civilisations and values. This was even considered as the progress of humanity. It is therefore not surprising to note today some scholars like Francis Fukuyama asserting that man has already reached the end of history and the final destiny of man has already arrived. In other words, it is the culmination of an era that was inaugurated by Vasco da Gama and Columbus in the fifteenth century.[24]

The noted American political scientist Samuel Huntington had put forward the theory that the world had entered into an era of 'Clash of Civilisations' with the demise of the Soviet Union. He asserted that future conflicts will be cultural and ethnic and not ideological as according to him capitalism which is an intrinsic part of western civilisation had triumphed over communism, which was also born in the west, as a reaction to capitalism.[25] But in the light of what I have pointed out, the world had entered a new era of 'Clash of Civilisations' right from the time Vasco da Gama stepped into Malabar and Columbus discovered America. This clash continued during the colonial period when the civilisation of the coloniser had the upper hand over the civilisation of the colonised and the values and ideologies of the coloniser in the political, economic and cultural fields were imposed upon the colonised. Samuel Huntington has failed to recognise adequately the fact that this new era of Clash of Civilisations had its origin long before in the fifteenth century when Vasco da Gama came to the Malabar Coast and Columbus stumbled upon America. The word 'civilisation' in my opinion involves all aspects of life and existence of a particular group of people at the political, religious, economic, cultural and ideological levels, unlike Huntington who tends to give it a cultural and ethnic meaning.

We know that the arrival of Vasco da Gama on the Malabar Coast was not a great exploit from the navigational point of view, as he just followed the course already charted by Portuguese navigators like Bartholomeu Diaz along the west African coast and then to cross the Arabian sea to Malabar from the east African coast, he took the help of a Muslim pilot. Then what was actually so great about Vasco da Gama that many historians highlight in their numerous books? Some Indian historians too subscribe to the greatness of Vasco da Gama. Is it because Vasco da Gama and his successors brought Christianity and Christian values to Malabar and India? Vasco da Gama under the orders of King D Manuel came to India definitely in order to proclaim Jesus Christ. But Christianity had come to India several centuries before Vasco da Gama's arrival and it was thriving particularly in Malabar during the fifteenth century. So Christianity and Christian values which were European values and part of European civilisation cannot account for the greatness of Vasco da Gama.

Apart from proclaiming Jesus Christ, Vasco da Gama had also orders to capture the wealth and lands of the barbarians, Moors, pagans and the other races. Vasco Da Gama and his successors implemented these orders to the best of their ability on the Malabar Coast and the Indian Ocean region, which was situated about 20000 miles away from their homelands, with the limited resources and numbers at their disposal. They acquired and captured lands at various points on the Malabar Coast, built formidable forts at vantage points, made Goa as their headquarters, indulged in proselytisation and even forcible conversions, mixed with the local populations to create a hybrid race who would be loyal to them and their values, controlled the Indian Ocean, imposed passes on Indian ships and monopolised trade on the Malabar coast to the detriment of Arab, Turkish, Persian, Indian, Chinese and Mappila traders.

All this they could do not because of their values or way of life, which they nevertheless sought to impose on others, but because of the sophisticated and superior arms and ammunitions that they possessed, especially in the form of guns and cannons. If they acquired a foothold on the Malabar Coast, in spite of their limited numbers, it was solely because of the arms that they had at their disposal and the better developed navigation vessels which were literally warships, fitted with bronze cannons and guns with which they could dominate ruthlessly the high seas and with which they could bombard and raze to the ground any coastal town, as it was the case with Calicut in 1502. It was this domination and power by the force of superior arms, capable of exterminating hundreds of people in one blow, which accounts largely for the greatness of Vasco da Gama and his successors and not because of their values or their intentions to trade or their navigational exploits, as it is made out to be generally by many modern historians. Besides it is wrong to contend that Vasco da Gama contributed to the meeting of the East and West. East and West had actually met several centuries earlier from the historical and geographical, cultural and racial point of views.

No other nation before the Portuguese had disrupted trade or had monopolised trade or had tried to monopolise trade in the Indian Ocean region. The Portuguese were followed by other west European nations like Denmark, Holland, England and France, who too had acquired more and more sophisticated arms and ammunitions and ocean-going vessels and warships. By the force of their arms and warships, they were powerful, though their nations were limited in size and numbers. With the help of their arms and warships they could impose their will not only in the Indian Ocean region but also in Malabar and in the Indian sub-continent and colonise and subjugate various and vast parts of the world and its people. Samuel Huntington himself had admitted that the west won the world not by the superiority of its ideas or values or religion, but rather by its superiority in applying organised violence. It would be ridiculous to maintain that the Europeans conquered and subjugated the world with their values and ideas. These values and ideas, which are not absolute scientific facts, came later. The arms, the cannonading and bombardment came first. The values and ideas came later to justify their actions and prolong their power and domination.

It is really unfortunate that scholars like Sanjay Subrahmanyam, coloured by their global vision of 'connected histories' had simply forgotten that the Portuguese were the inaugurators of 'gun-boat trade and politics' in the region and the perpetrators of what we may term as the 'confrontational history' in south Asia and the Indian Ocean region. They had laid the foundation for this confrontation, which resulted in a violent and unequal relationship between the Europeans and the peoples of Malabar and Hindustan right from the beginning.

This relationship took the form of colonisation, which is nothing but an improved version of slavery, where the colonisers were always the masters, while the colonised were the 'petted slaves', and where the earlier indigenous self-sustaining cooperative village economies was subjected in the course of time to a certain centralised, colonial, competitive, capitalist, machine-based economy and civilisation of western origin. Capitalism is an intrinsic and dominant part of western civilisation and culture as it was born in Western Europe where the capitalists by first controlling the means of production and the produce reduced a vast number of people to the status of workers. This civilisation had naturally spread to India or struck root in India during the colonial period. Capitalism is not just an economic phenomenon. It has also a political and cultural side to it, in which it thrives. It generates its own permissive culture, in the place of other cultures or in opposition to other cultures. It is actually a whole way of life which is the western or modern way of life. This way of life is fundamentally violent as it is based on Darwinian theories of competition and the selection of the fittest. Western culture and capitalism is almost inseparable. It is sheer naivety to oppose western culture without getting rid of capitalism, which is in essence the concentration of power in the hands of the few and their political allies and the subordination of the vast mass of people to them. This subordination, which is an improved version of slavery, is generally masked or hidden by the general term 'progress' as well as by the massive entertainment industry like television, internet, sports and cinema. Even sex, the only giver of life and therefore sacred, if one thinks that life is sacred, has been reduced to a pleasure industry and entertainment by the capitalists and their protagonists.

It is quite astonishing to note that Sheikh Zainuddin living in the late sixteenth century had understood perfectly well the inseparability of Portuguese culture and monopolist economics when he chose to oppose both tooth and nail through his work. He condemned not only Portuguese permissiveness and moral depravity, under cover of Christianity, but also their extremely violent and inhuman streak in order to impose their economic and political domination over the Hindu Zamorin Raja of Malabar and his Mappila allies as well as the entire Indian Ocean region. He was the first to envisage through his work a clash of civilisations unfolding between the Portuguese and the Zamorin's subjects.

In 1909 in Hind Swaraj, Mahatma Gandhi using the words of Prophet Mohammad called this western way of life or civilisation as the 'Satanic Civilisation'. But this 'Satanic civilisation' of Gandhi did not end with the departure of the colonialists from India in 1947 because the economic and political power structures and systems put in place by the colonisers were maintained and even amplified by the successive authorities, who took over power from the colonial authorities, paving the way for the westernisation of the Indian society.

The present 'globalisation' offensive, launched by capitalist interests of the west and their power-wielding allies and protagonists, is a sequel to the colonialist offensive of yesteryears. This western offensive is not just economic, but also political and cultural. The launchers, driven most certainly by the pathology of the urge to dominate, seem to assume that they know better than the vast diverse multitude of more than six billion human beings about what is good for every single man or woman on this earth and how they should behave or evolve. They go about preaching or imposing their values, way of life and ideas, which they think is right and reasonable on the others who do not share their views, through propaganda, persuasion, arguments, force, coercion, technology, economic power, legislation, international organisations and the numbers game, destroying in the process all individual and collective creativity, intelligence and freedom as well as the natural diversity of the human race, in favour of a single, monotonous, narrow and coercive political, economic and cultural system. This strait-jacket system, fashioned by power-hungry megalomaniacs, has reduced humanity into just two blatantly and profoundly unequal categories viz., a handful of capitalists and their powerful elite allies on the top and an overwhelming huge mass of graded salaried and toiling classes below them, both held together by the same political ideology. This is considered by the globalists, who aim for indefinite global control over the lives of all human beings, as the ultimate 'progress' that man can achieve, beyond which they believe that there is nothing. The capitalist system by its very nature and competitive structure is the generator of inequality, corruption and unethical behaviour. It does not care of whether one believes in God or does not believe in God. It does not care if one believes in One God or in ten thousand gods. It does not care if one sleeps with one woman or man or with ten women or men. It has caused the destruction of the environment, forests, plant species, animal, bird and aquatic species, within a space of just two centuries or so of its existence. It has caused immense pollution of air, water and earth. 'Progress' and science which were supposed to cure all diseases have ended up in the multiplication of diseases. Hospitals are overflowing with sick people. The scientists have no answer to diseases, old age and death, which were and are still the fundamental problems of man. They and their sponsors promise heaven in a distant future in the planets like Mars and so on. But they cannot solve the fundamental problems of man. Inequality has widened more than ever before. Where there is inequality, there is bound to be injustice. But capitalism and capitalists and their protagonists do not care. Their overriding interest is to make profits, with the intention of dominating the other. It is quite strange to note that the secularists, who consider themselves to be more progressive than the non-secularists were historically tied up or feel more comfortable with capitalism or its Marxian and non-Marxian offshoots in one way or the other. It is sheer naivety or ignorance and a monstrous lie to think or continue to think and make others think that one can reform the capitalist system and make it more human and egalitarian. It has not happened anywhere in the world since the birth and evolution of capitalism as the core of western culture and civilisation some two hundred years ago. However all the preceding would not have probably come about if the Indian and Malabar powers had heeded to the lonely passionate call of Sheikh Zainuddin and had come to the aid of the Hindu Zamorin Raja of Calicut and his Marakkar and Nair warriors, in evincing the Portuguese from the Malabar Coast and the Indian Ocean in the sixteenth century which would have changed the course of Indian and world history. But that was not to be.

Before I end this note, I would like to draw the attention of the reader to the fact that Sheikh Zainuddin's work was a rare sixteenth century historical document of universal importance which deals with the colonisation and the attempts at colonisation of India and the Eastern world by the Europeans since the arrival of Vasco da Gama and the Portuguese on the Malabar coast. It is one of the world's pioneering documents written in impeccable literary style which recount in all its details the atrocities that the Malabaris underwent at the hands of the Portuguese colonisers. It also recounts the valiant efforts made by the Hindu Zamorin of Calicut and his Malabar Muslim and Nair warriors to stop European colonial expansion in India and the Eastern world. It stands testimony to the beginning of a new era of clash of civilisations and values and to the defining moments that changed the course of history. This is a document which allows the reader to experience the context and situation when the foundation for the subjugation and the colonisation of India and the world were being laid by the west Europeans by the force of their arms and ammunitions. As a neutral and uncommitted historian, with no ethnic, linguistic, religious or ideological moorings, I am happy to present to the reader this monumental work of the Sheikh of Malabar, in its English version as translated from the original Arabic by the illustrious British Arabic-Persian scholar M.J. Rowlandson.

N tes

1. K.M. Panikkar, *Asia and Western Dominance: A Survey of the Vasco da Gama epoch in Asian History, 1498-1947*, London, 1959; Ashin Das Gupta, 'Indian Merchants in the Age of Partnership, c. 1500-1800' (in) Uma Das Gupta, ed. *The World of the Indian Ocean Merchant. Collected Essays of Ashin Das Gupta*, New Delhi, 2001, pp. 243-245; Sanjay Subrahmanyam, 'Introduction', (in) Uma Das Gupta, ed. *The World of the Indian Ocean Merchant. Collected Essays of Ashin Das Gupta*, New Delhi, 2001, p. 6

2. M.J. Rowlandson, tr. & ed. *Tohfut-al-mujahideen* by Sheikh Zeen-ud-deen, London, 1833

3. Elliot & Dowson, ed. *The History of India as told by its own Historians*, I, India, 1867, pp. 2, 3, 18-25, 85, 89, 90, 95

4. JBP.More. *Origin and Early History of the Muslims of Keralam, 700 AD to 1600 AD*, Calicut, 2011, ch.4

5. E. Tisserant, *Eastern Christianity in India*, London, 1957, p. 29; F.C. Danvers, *The Portuguese in India*, I, London, 1894, xxxvi, 21, 39fn; Sir George Birdwood, *Report on the Old Records of the India Office*, Calcutta, 1891, p. 113; C.R. Boxer, *The Portuguese Sea-borne empire, 1415-1815*, London, 1969, pp. 20-25

6. Cf. Ma Huan, Ying-Yai Sheng-Lan. *The Overall Survey of the Ocean's Shores*, 1433, Bangkok, 1970, pp. 10-19, 138; JBP.More, *op.cit.* pp. 83-85

7. EG. Ravenstein, tr. & ed. *A Journal of the First Voyage of Vasco da Gama, 1497-1499*, London, 1898, pp. 157-165, 173-174, 178-179; Glenn J. Ames, *Em Nome De Deus: The Journal of the First Voyage of Vasco da Gama to India, 1497-1499*, Leiden, 2009, pp. 6, 7, 9-14, 16, 17, 29, 30, 125, 126; KG. Jayne, Vasco da Gama and His Successors, 1460-1580, London, 1910, ch.V; Sanjay Subrahmanyam, *The Career and Legend of Vasco da Gama*, Cambridge, 1997,

p. 79; F.C. Danver, op.cit. p. 50

8. Sir George Birdwood, *op.cit.* p. 162; EG. Ravenstein, *Ibid.* p. 44; Glenn Ames, *Ibid.* pp. 23, 24, 51, 52, 53, 66, 67; KG. Jayne, *Ibid.* pp. 42, 43; 48

9. JBP.More, *op.cit.* pp. 155-160

10. EG. Ravenstein, *op.cit.* pp. xx, xxii, 113-128; Glenn Ames, *op.cit.* pp. 18-29 ; JBP.More, *Ibid.* p. 162

11. Sir George Birdwood, *op.cit.* p. 165; G. Bouchon, *Regent of the Sea: Cannanore's Response to Portuguese Expansion 1507-1528,* Delhi, 1988, p. 52; Glenn Ames, *op.cit.* p. 163; JBP. More, *Ibid.* pp. 162-163

12. KG. Jayne, *op.cit.* pp. 192, 285-286; JBP.More, *Ibid.* p. 178

13. Anthony Disney, *'Vasco da Gama's Reputation for Violence': Alleged Atrocities at Calicut in 1502',* Indica, 32, 2, 1995, pp. 12-28; Glenn Ames, *op.cit.* p. 167; Stephen Dale, *Islamic Society in the South Asian Frontier,* Oxford, 1980, pp. 35, 38; JBP.More, *Ibid.* pp. 101, 164-165; Tomé Pires, *Sumo Oriental of Tomé Pires, 1512-1515,* Nendeln, 1967, pp. 77-78; K.S. Mathew, *Portuguese and the Sultanate of Gujarat (1500-1573),* Delhi, 1986, pp. 100-101

14. Stephen Dale, *Ibid.* pp. 3, 52, 53; Sir George Birdwood, *op.cit.* p. 181; KG. Jayne, *op.cit.* p. 65; JBP.More, *Ibid.* pp. 166-169

15. M.J. Rowlandson, *Ibid;* Sanjay Subrahmanyam, *The Portuguese Expansion in Asia, 1500-1700. A Political and Economic History,* London, 1993, pp. 55-56

16. JBP.More, op.cit. p. 166; JBP.More, *'Hindu-Christian Interaction in Pondicherry, 1700-1900',* Contributions to Indian Sociology, 32, 1, 1998, pp. 97-122

17. M.J. Rowlandson, op.cit; K.S. Latourette, *The History of the Expansion of Christianity,* III, New York, 1971, pp. 249-255; JBP.More, *Ibid.* 2011, pp. 168-169

18. Gopinatha Rao, *'Extracts from the Mushaka Vamsam and 'Mushakavamsa: A Study',* Travancore Archaelogical series, II,I, no.10, pp. 87-113; *Annemarie Schimmel, Islamic Literatures of India,* Wiesbaden, 1973, pp. 4-5

19. JBP.More *Ibid.,* p. 135

20. The author had personally visited the tomb of Sheikh Zainuddin at Chombala, near Mahé

21. Ashin Das Gupta, 'Indian Merchants in the Age of Partnership, c. 1500-1800', *Ibid*, pp. 243-245; Ashin Das Gupta, 'Europeans in India before the Empire', *Ibid.*, 2001, p. 226; Ashin Das Gupta, *Merchants of Maritime India, 1500-1800*, Hampshire, 1994, p. 93; Sanjay Subrahmanyam, 'Introduction', *op.cit.*, p. 6

22. JBP.More, *op.cit.* pp. 173-176

23. M.N. Pearson, *'The Portuguese in India and the Indian Ocean: An Overview of the 16th Century'*, (in) *Kerala Spectrum; Aspects of Cultural Inheritance*, ed. by Charles Dias, Cochin, 2006, pp. 197-198; Sanjay Subrahmanyam, *Ex plorations in Connected History. From the Tagus to the Ganges*, New Delhi, 2005

24. Charles Darwin, *On the Origin of Species*, Cambridge, 1966; Charles Darwin, *The Descent of Man and Selection in Rela tion to Sex*, London, 1871; Francis Fukuyama, *The End of History and the Last Man*, New York, 1992

25. Samuel Huntington, *The Clash of Civilizations and the Remaking of World Order*, New York, 1996

M.J.Rowlandson's Preface

Of Sheikh Zeen-ud-deen, the author of the Tohfut-ul-mujahideen, but little appears known. From that work we learn, that he lived in the reign of Sultan Ali Adil Shah, the fifth sovereign of the Adil Shahi dynasty of Bijapur: whilst from his title of "Al-maburee",[1] it may be concluded that he was a descendant of one of the original inhabitants from Arabia; but beyond these points, no information regarding him appears to exist. Ferishta, the only author from whom any account of him might be expected, in stating, that the brief account of Malabar[2] to be found in his general History of Hindustan, was chiefly taken from the Tohfut-ul-mujahideen, is altogether silent upon the subject of the authorship of that work; a silence remarkable, when it is considered that Sheikh Zeen-ud-deen and himself must have been contemporary historians, or nearly so; and at the same court, as his (Ferishta's) introduction at the court of Bijapur took place, according to his own account, in the year of the Hegira 998, or ten years only after the assasination[3] of Ali Adil Shah, to whom the Sheikh Zeen-ud-deen dedicated the original of this translation.

In this selection of his patron, the author of the Tohfut-ul-mujahideen was induced, he tells us, by the unwearied zeal and activity which Ali Adil Shah had displayed[4] in warning against infidels, to excite his Mahomedan brethren generally, but more particularly those in power, to a more vigorous resistance of the Christian heretics, who had invaded the possessions of the faithful in the countries of Malabar, constituting his avowed object in the compilation of his narrative.

That these Christian infidels, although described by the Sheikh under the general title of "Al-Afrunj," or the Franks, were the

Portuguese, it is hardly necessary to remark. That he was not, however, more particular in his denomination of these deadly enemies of his race(as he would have them) it is hard to imagine, if the fact that, although Abul-feda in his Universal History (written in the fourteenth century), is found to distinguish Richard Coeur de Lion by the title of "Al Inkitar," or, the Englishman; yet that this title (like those of Al Andaloos and Al-Afransawee, for the Spaniard and the Frenchman) was only of late years become familiar amongst the Mahomedans of India, who formerly applied to the English, French, and Portuguese, indiscriminately, the title of "Al-Afrunj" – shall not be considered to account for it.

   With a view to throw light on what follows, the author has prefixed to his narrative of the earlier proceedings of the Portuguese in Malabar in three introductory chapters. In the first of these, he recounts the several commands of Mahomed to his followers to exterminate infidelity; dilating also upon the meritorious nature and ultimate reward of that act of religious duty. Here the Sheikh, after the manner of Peter the Hermit (his object, however, being directly opposed to that which animated the wandering preacher of the Crusades), would endeavour to excite his brethren to a holy war against the infidel intruders – the cursed "Franks". The second chapter purports to be an account of the first dissemination of the Mohamedan religion in Malabar. In the third, the author would describe the singular usages and customs which distinguish the Nairs and other inhabitants of that country.

   With this introduction, the account of the proceedings of the Portuguese is commenced from the time of their first arrival in Malabar (which event is fixed by the author of the Tohfut-ul-mujahideen in the middle of the year of the Hijra 904[5]), and is continued up to the Mahomedan year 985[6]; the narrative thus embracing a period of between eighty and ninety years. That the Sheikh is not here upon untroddden ground will be obvious. The action of de Gama, the great Portuguese navigator, who ranks only second to his greater contemporary Columbus, have been immortalized by his countryman Camoens ("Le Virgile des Portugais," as Voltaire had styled him), in his poem of "Os Lusiades, or The Lusiad," a poem familiar to the English reader, by the elegant version of Mickle; whilst in the Portuguese histories of Maffeius, Osorius, Barros and Faria-y-Souza, the exploits of Cabral, Albuquerque, Almeida, and their successors in India, have been celebrated with great diffuseness. It is creditable to the Sheikh, that the testimony of these authors establishes the fidelity of his narrative; since, besides a very minute and extraordinary agreement, on many minor points of detail, in the relation of leading events, it is seldom found much at variance with their accounts. In the voluminous work of Maffeius, written under royal authority and expressly "celebrate domestica facta" this agreement is more particularly remarkable, as will be seen by the quotations from that writer which will be met with in the historical or latter part of this translation.

Intruders themselves, the Mahomedans naturally regarded the Portuguese, who came in a like character, with feelings of jealousy and mistrust; and from the Portuguese histories we find, that De Gama and his successors early entertained a no common degree of animosity and dislike towards these "Saracens" as they termed them. Under these circumstances, it is not to be expected that, in judging of the natives which actuated the actions of their respective countrymen, the Mahomedan and his Catholic contemporaries should much agree. It must be confessed that they do not; and more, that were it not for the evidence to his credibility above alluded to, which secures of him from such a change, the Sheikh, from his frequent and hearty imprecations of evil upon "these cursed Franks" (as he syles them), might have been suspected of having mixed up his feelings with his narrative, to the prejudice of its truth. Upon the subject of this want of courtesy, on the part of our author, if any apology can be admissible for such an offence in one setting himself up for an historian, it may be remarked, that the furious and persecuting spirit which the Portuguese invariably displayed throughout their Indian rule, was felt by no class of men more severely than the Mahomedan merchants of Malabar; and further, that the cruelties ascribed by him to the Portuguese, fall far short of the atrocious acts which writers of their own country and religion have admitted as justly chargeable to them. The translator would here particularly refer to the account, by Monsieur Dellon, of the Inquisition of Goa (written about one hundred and fifty years ago), where a picture is shown of that diabolical institution much more highly coloured than the Sheikh's description of that "house of darkness and stench'", the terms which he uses when speaking of it. In the work of Fra Paolino, also, no attempt has been made to conceal or deny the barbarities practised by his countrymen in the East. As on this point, therefore (one on which he might have been expected to exaggerate), the Sheikh appears to have been guilty of no exaggeration, it is not unreasonable to suppose, that in general his account of the tyrannical and oppressive conduct of the Portuguese whilst in Malabar, is not withdrawn. It would be inexcusable in the translator to lengthen further his remarks upon so inconsiderable a performance, and he will therefore only add the expression of his hopes, that the inelegancies of language and style, which have been inseparable from a close adherence to his author (his object having been to give a liberal and faithful version), will be overlooked; also, of his acknowledgements to the gentleman[7] by whose kindness he became possessed of the original M.S.; and to Mr.J.Lushington, the Secretary of the Madras Auxiliary Branch of the Royal Asiaitic Society, whose readiness to assist persons engaged in works of the description now offercd, keeps pace with his ability to do it, and to whom the translator was indebted, besides the loan of a copy, for much valuable information regarding the original of this translation.

Notes:

1. "one passed over, an emigrant"
2. This account written in the Persian language was some years ago translated into English by Mr.Anderson, and lately by Colonel Briggs, in his improved version of Ferishta's General History. It consists chiefly of extracts from that part of the Tohfut-ul-mujahideen which relates to the propagation of the Mahomedan religion in Malabar, and of a brief summary of the historical part of that work; but as the whole chapter (of Ferishta) does not

exceed twelve pages, this last is necessarily imperfect; whilst to the existence of a considerable portion of the work, the Persian historian has made no allusion.

3. A.D.1579. He was assassinated by a eunuch, under circumstances which, for many years, were considered mysterious but which are now sufficiently well known to reflect much infamy upon Alee-adil Shah's memory.

4. The author may be supposed here chiefly to allude to the share which Alee-adil took in the destruction of Ramraj, the Rai of Vijayanagar, in the year 1565. His alliance, however, with that infidel and unfortunate chieftain, only a few years before, against a Moslem prince (Nizam Shah of Ahmednagar), the Sheikh would appear either to have forgiven or forgotten.

5. Here agreeing entirely with the Portuguese accounts of the arrival of Vasco Da Gama at Calicut, in May 1498.

6. In what may be considered as a postscript to the work, some account of the condition of the Portuguese in Malabar, up to the year 1581, has been given. As this last date, however, is two years after the assassination of Alee-adil Shah (to whom Tohfut-ul-mujahideen is described) the translator must conclude that this is not from the pen of Sheikh Zein-ud-deen; as, had it been added by him subsequently, he could hardly have avoided some allusion to that event.

7. The Hon.W.Oliver, member of Council, Fort St.George

4

Sheikh Zainuddin's Preface
With notes by M.J.Rowlandson

In the Name of God, The All Merciful and All Compassionate!

All praise and thanksgiving be ascribed to God! Who in revealing the religion of Islam, exalted it above all creeds, having blessed with his divine favour all who have embraced it, from the early ages until now.[1] And blessing and peace to His Prophet (he who is the true way to that faith which shall endure forever!) and upon his posterity and companions[2], on all of them! For the God (hallowed be His name) has mercifully distinguished His servants having vouchsafed to them discrimination, judgement, and wisdom; and multiplied to them all things necessary; having brought to light that which leadeth to salvation, and to the attainment of all excellence; further having sent unto them prophets, who were the bearers of good tidings, and who by exhortation gave knowledge of the Lord, directing in the right way. But, chiefly, are we indebted to the divine goodness, in that we have been born of the race of the choice of his created beings, Mahomed (upon whom the blessing and peace of God for ever rest!), herein being raised above all nations. The Lord most high hath said, " Ye are the chosen race, selected from among mankind;"[3] and, declared the Prophet of God (with whom may the divine favour ever dwell!) " I am a prince of the race of Adam, and the most exalted."[4]

And, if it be true that he (on whom be peace) was the lord of the posterity of Adam, it followed that he was super-excellent above the whole, and the super-excellence of his descendants is a consequence of the super-excellence of himself.

Further the Imam Ahmad[5] has related upon the authority of Al-Mikdad[6] (on whom be peace) that he heard the Prophet (for ever blessed) to exclaim: "There shall not remain a dwelling in the city, or in the plain, on which the Lord shall not cause to descend the word of Islam, which shall dignify him already righteous and condemn him who lives in sin, to the salvation of the one, and the everlasting ruin of the other." For those whom "God would exalt," will he make of the number of true believers, whilst those whose destruction has been pre-determined, shall seal it by rejecting this holy faith, which indeed, " said I, "has god for its author and its end." Now be it known that the Lord most high hath willed, that the faith of Islam should flourish throughout the chief of the inhabited regions of the earth; in some countries making the sword and compulsion the means of its dissemination, in others preaching and exhortation. But he mercifully ordained that the people of Malabar, beyond the other nations of India, should evince a ready and willing acceptance of the holy creed; their profession of it being void of monastic guile and free from distrust. The occasion of their conversion was as follows:

A Company of Moslems having emigrated to certain ports of Malabar,[7] and subsequently there taken up their dwelling, the population by degrees became proselytes to the religion of God; and Islam shedding abroad its divine lustre, the number of its professors became increased. And these building for themselves in that quarter, and abstaining from all oppression towards the idolatrous populace, and from any interference with them in the exercise of their ancient customs (under the divine protection) lived in happiness and prosperity. Enjoying this prosperity for a season, but having by infidelity forfeited the favour of the Almighty, and rebelled against, and set themselves at variance to the Divine authority, God raised up against them the nations of Europe, the Franks – whom may the Most High eternally confound! And these beginning to oppress and commit hostilities against the Mahomedans, their tyrannical and injurious usage[8] proceeded to a length that was the occasion of a general confusion and distraction amongst the population of the country. This continued for a long period, for nearly eighty years, when the affairs of the Muslims had arrived at the last stage of decay, ruin, poverty and wretchedness;

since, whilst they were too ill practised in deceit to dissemble an obedience which was not sincere, they neither possessed the power to repel, nor means to evade, the evils that afflicted them. Nor did the Mahomedan princes and chieftains who were possessed of large armies, and who had at their command great military resources, at all came forward for their deliverance, or bestow any of their wealth in so holy a cause as in the resistance of these tyrant infidels; seeing that, for the most part, they were indifferent towards the interests of their religion[9] and unwilling to barter their worldly wealth for an eternal reward. For this cause, therefore, have I compiled this narrative; having in view, the arousing of the faithful to engage in a holy warfare against the worshippers of crucifixes, that they should engage in it, being a duty of divine command, these infidels having invaded territories inhabited by Mahomedans, and having taken prisoners from them a multitude whose number cannot be computed; having also put many of the faithful to death, and compelled a vast body of them to embrace Christianity; and lastly, made captives of their females, and when bound and in shackles, having violated their persons, in this manner causing Christian children to be brought into being, who also have in after time occupied themselves in aggressions and injuries against the faithful; and in tyrannically oppressing them. Now, touching the title of this work, I have styled it "Tohfut-ul-mujahideen,"[10] or an offering to warriors who shall fight in "defence of religion against infidels;" it being the history of the affairs of the Franks in the countries of Malabar, and recounting their infamous machinations against the religion of Islam. Furthermore, I have shown in this work, the great reward that shall await those who shall engage in hostilities against infidels like these; having added also, an exhortation to that act of religious duty, and which has been chiefly taken from the sacred writings.

In the Tohfut-ul-mujahideen also will be found some account of the customs that distinguish the Pagans of Malabar. And I have compiled this history as an offering for the gracious acceptance of the most glorious of Sultans, and the most beneficent of monarchs, who has made war against infidels the chief act of his life, having himself glorified God and made his name to be upheld with reverence by all; having ever devoted himself to the service and the protection of the servants of God, and exerted himself with praiseworthy zeal in destroying his enemies, giving animation to the divine faith, and extirpate all who would disseminate heresy in the kingdom of God. One who is the uniform cherisher of the learned and the good, and the firm protector of the poor and destitute; a prince overruling the destinies and fates of the powerful at all times and reasons; who, notwithstanding his youth has arrived at the highest dignities, and notwithstanding the machinations of his enemies, to the most permanent honours; whose whole nature is composed of generosity and virtue; the fame of whose virtues has diffused its odour throughout the world; whose sway supersedes that of all other monarchs, the kings of Arabia and Persia dwindling into insignificance when compared to him; the golden shower of whose generosity descends upon the learned of distant lands; a monarch of great humanity, whose clemency surpasses that of all who have gone before him; victorious in arms, invincible, reflecting splendours upon the needs of former days; one whose exploits form the theme of assemblies and the topic of great cities, whose acts of liberality are emblazoned forth throughout the land, who strenuously had laboured, to destroy infidelity and to root out idleness; withal, a firm maintainer of justice and mercy, opening the palm of benevolence and favour; - the mighty and gracious monarch, the Sultan Alee-adil Shah! May God exalt, by means of his perfections, the commands of His religion, and establish them! May he use him as His instrument for the destruction of all that are rebellious and wicked, and give him the victory over all who are his enemies; extending his dominion throughout the universe, from the east to the west, and granting to him the sovereignty whether by land or by sea, whether in Persia or in Arabia. The Imam to whose virtuous qualities Khafee Khan[11] has given his testimony; in whose service the powerful willingly enlist themselves, perceiving his innate estimation for men of virtue and probity, and that, on account of their observance of the law, he bestowing upon them both dignities and honour. May God, most high, ever perpetuate throughout the world his grace and integrity, by prolonging his life, and by granting mankind to enjoy the benefit of their exercise, through the blessing of Mahomed and his posterity!

To conclude, the work is divided into four chapters. The first, treating of certain divine commands, wherein war against infidels is enjoined, and also of the future rewards that awaits those who shall engage in it, being designed as an exhortation to arms in this cause. The second, of the early promulgation of Islam in the countries of Malabar. The third, of the most singular of the customs of the Pagans of Malabar. The fourth, of the arrival of the Franks in the countries of Malabar; relating also certain of their detestable acts there. And this chapter is again divided into sections. The first of these giving an account of the earliest appearance of the Franks in Malabar, and of the hostility that arose between them and the Moslems and the Samree;[12] also of their conciliating the Rajahs of Kushee[13] and Kuzhangaloor,[14] and erecting forts at those places and at Kolum;[15] lastly, of their seizure of the port of Goa. The second section contains a narrative of certain of their infamous proceedings. The third, an account of their treaty with the Zamorin, and of their proceeding to construct fortifications at Calicut. The fourth relates the differences that shortly after took place between them and the Zamorins, and gives an account of the capture of the forts which they had built. The fifth is regarding the accommodation that the Franks for the second time entered into with the Zamorin, relating also their building fortifications at Shalleat.[16] The sixth tells us of the third treaty and league entered into between the Franks and the Zamorin. The seventh, of the compact of the great Sultan[17] Bahadur Shah Ben Muzuffur, of Guzerat, entered into with them, and of his delivering over to them many of the principle ports of his kingdom. The eighth, of the arrival of Pasha Soliman, vizier of the great sultan soliman-Shah of Room,[18] both now no more (peace to their spirits), at Diu[19] and in its vicinity; and of the return of the former to Egypt, he having been unsuccessful in the object of his expedition. The ninth recounts the treaty between Franks and the Zamorin, entered into for the fourth time. The tenth, the differences which again fell out between the Franks and the Zamorin. The eleventh, the treaty entered into between the Franks and the Zamorin for the fifth time. The twelfth, the occasion of a renewal of hostilities between the Zamorin and the Franks; giving an account, also, of the sailing forth of a fleet of grabs (belonging to that chief) to attack them. The thirteenth relates the capture of this fort, their earnest desire and great efforts for the subversion of the religion of Islam, and the ruin of the Mohamedans in the countries of Malabar.

Notes:

1. With a view of conveying to the English reader some idea of the style of the Tohfut-ul-mujahideen, the translator in rendering into English these introductory pages of his author, has left the construction of the sentences entirely as they are found in the original Arabic.

2. Although the author would here establish his orthodoxy, by including the "Sahibeh," or the three first Caliphs, Omar, Aboobakur and Othman in his benedictions, yet from the tenets of his patron having been notoriously otherwise (one of the first acts of Ali Adil Shah, upon his succeeding to the throne of Bijapur, having been to denounce the Sahibeh, and to adopt the doctrines of the Shia sect), it seems justly subject to some suspicion.

   During the lifetime of his father Ibrahim Adil Shah, his son Ali (Ferishta tells us) discovered his attachment to the tenets of Abu-Talib. The Sheikh therefore, it must be concluded, was either a very tolerant Sunni (the orthodox sect), or what perhaps is more probable, himself one of those who held heterodox opinions regarding the Sunnah or Book of the Prophet's traditions.

3. Koran, Surah "Imran" (in the third chapter) a name which Mahomed has given to the father of Virgin Mary. In this chapter an account is given of the birth of Jesus Christ and of John the Baptist, very similar to that recorded by the Evangelists. As usual, however, Mahomed is not contented with relating the matter as he found it, but is guilty of one of his blasphemous and childish interpolations, in which he causes our Saviour to animate a bird that he had made of clay.

Note: The preceding shows that the translator M.J.Rowlandoson was an ardent Christian, well-versed with the Bible as well as the Koran, which pushes him to find fault with Prophet Mohammad.

4. This is a quotation for the Sooheih Bukharee, a collection of traditions regarding Mahomed, very similar to the "Sooheih Mooselim."

5. Or Al-Ghazzali, one of the most celebrated of the commentators upon the Koran. He was born in the year of the Hegira 450 or A.D.1060. In consequence of his great repute for learning, he was styled Imam-al-allum, the Imam of the World. His chief work was "Ahia aloom-ad-deen," or a disquisition upon the sciences connected to religion.

6. One of the associates of Mahomed. In modern days, Muslims divide the Prophet's associates into two great classes: 1. The Al Ansar (the aiders); 2. Al Muhajerien (those who fled), being those who accompanied Prophet Mahomed in his flight into Abyssinia.

7. The emigrants from Arabia in the reign of Hijaj-Ben-Yusuf, A.D.710. These, who at this time, under the Caliph V a l i d , established in Malabar, may be considered the ancestors of the Mahomedans of southern India, who are in this day commonly called Moors; whilst the Pathans or Afghans are said to be a branch of the Albanians, from the Mount Caucasus.

8. The excesses of the Portuguese will be found detailed at length in the historical or later part of this work. They have formed a subject for the pens of writers of all nations; amongst others, the great English dramatist, Cumberland:

"With avarice and ambition fir'd,
 Eager alike for plunder and for fame,
Onward they press to spring upon their prey.
There every spoil obtained, with greedy haste
By force or fraud could ravish from the hands
Of nature's peaceful sons, again they mount
Their richly frighted bark. She, while the cries
Of widows and of orphans rend the strand,
Striding the billows, to the venal winds
Spreads her broad vans, and flies before the gale."

- Historical Fragments

9. It would seem from the histories of the courts of Bijapur, Ahmednagar and Golconda (to which courts the Sheikh here would chiefly allude), that at the time of the arrival of the Portuguese in India, these powers were too much occupied in their own intrigues and quarrels to regard with much interest or concern the proceedings of "a handful of foreign vagabonds," as the historians of that day would describe them. It was not until the year 1570 that Adil Shah made his first (unsuccessful) attempt to recover Goa.

10. "Tohfut-ul-mujahideen." "Tohfut" a present, offering; "Mujahideen", plural oblique of "Mujahid", active principle of Jihad, quadrilateral infinitive; he fought against "infidels," holy warfare. Actually the title of "Tohfut" is prefixed to several Arabic and Persian works.

11. Writer of a voluminous history in the Persian language.

12. This chief, who is called Zamorin, or Samorin, by Europeans was the Rajah of Calicut. At the time of the arrival of the Portuguese in India he was one of the most powerful of the princes of Malabar, having early entered into a league with the Arabs, who had established themselves at Calicut, against his powerful neighbour, the Rajah of Cochin, Perampadapil, or "Trimumpara", as Maffeus styles him. The ruling passion of this monarch (according to the Portuguese historians) was avarice. His chief revenue was derived from the traffic of the Moors, and he at first eagerly derived a commercial intercourse with the Portuguese.

13. Cochin

14. Cranganore

15. Quilon

16. Or Jalleat, as Ferishta calls it

17. The eighth in succession of the kings of Guzerat. He was killed in an affray with the Portuguese A.D.1527

18. The Turkish Empire, or Ottoman Empire

19. An island of the southern extremity of the province of Guzerat

Chapter I

Regarding certain divine commands[1] wherein war against infidels is required. Treating, also, of the reward that shall await that act of religious duty, and being designed as an exhortation to it.

Know then, that infidels shall be regarded in two distinct points of view. And first: those who are dwelling peaceably in their own countries, and against whom if one person only from any party of Moslems shall go forth to war, the divine command on this subject will have been sufficiently observed,[2] and the remainder of his brethren are not called upon to proceed against them. But should no one be found thus to offer himself as the holy champion of his party, then it becomes the duty of all to arm.

Secondly: The case of infidels who shall invade the territories of the Moslems, as is now the case in the contest in which we are engaged.[3] Now to attack these, becomes our act of paramount duty for every pious Mahomedan, and for all who would support their religion, whether bond or free, male or female, of the city or of the plains, without being dependent on or guided by the consent or refusal of master, husband, father or creditor, or of any other person to whom he or she might in other matters owe obedience; since to engage in this warfare is imperative on every person, whether within three[4] day's journey of the position of the infidels or beyond that distance; should the forces of the faithful not be sufficiently strong to admit of their services being dispensed with.[5] It is the duty of him who is the leader in this holy war to take counsel, and concert measures, with his companions, regarding the manner in which hostilities should be carried on, setting in order their ranks; and, should any plunder fall into their hands, first causing it to be collected into in one place, and afterwards distributing it, giving the effects of the slain to those by whose swords they fell. And, regarding this subject of the division of booty[6], whatever shall have been the personal property of the infidel (for instance, his clothes, boots, waistbelt, purse of money, or any cash or portion of his pay, or rings of silver or gold that shall be found in his person, with his weapons and horse, and saddle and bridle), of all these the chief shall make an equal division into five shares. Of these shares, one being again divided by him into five portions. And of these portions, one shall be set aside for the general good of the Muslims, to be appropriated in the repairing of breaches, the building of fortifications and bridges, the raising of mosques, and for defraying the salaries of Kazis and Imams. Another shall be given to the descendants of the Prophet (upon whom be the blessing and peace of God!), to the descendants[7] of Hashum and the descendants of Motalleb. One portion shall be distributed amongst those who are orphans and one amongst the poor and destitute, in whose number the fakers shall be included. The fifth portion shall go to the travellers.[8] And the four shares out of five that remain shall be the property of the captors and those who were present at the time of the battle, and who actually were engaged in it. Further, he who combats against infidels, should offer up prayers and supplication to God for victory; occupying himself in the performance of acts of piety, reposing especially the whole trust in God (most high!), before engaging in this holy warfare, for God it is who makes to prosper. Also he should beware of being guilty of any fraud or perfidy in the division of the plunder, against which there exist awful threatenings. Now it should be known, that from the Mahomedans of Malabar having no emir[9] amongst them, who possessed of sufficient power and authority to govern them and to watch over their interests, they in consequence paid allegiance to the pagans. Notwithstanding this, however, engaging in hostilities against the (Christian) infidels, and freely expending their substance in warring against them, each according to the extent of his means; being assisted in this warfare by that friend of the Mahomedans the Zamorin,[10] and being enabled to carry on hostilities against them, by his distribution to them of money and of warlike equipments generally; this warfare having been early commenced upon by the Mahomedans, and having been persevered in by them, until their own condition in Malabar had become ; eatly reduced, in consequence of the interruption to their trade aⁱd the sacrifice of life and devastation of property, to which they had, in consequence of such a course, subjected themselves. Indeed, by their resolute adherence to it, their necessities becoming every day more urgent, so that shortly they had arrived at the last stage of poverty, and decay, and wretchedness. Nor in this their distress did the neighbouring Mahomedan princes, or their emirs, evince any commiseration towards them, (nevertheless may God bless all those who shall afford them succour!) although to engage in this sacred warfare was incumbent upon them. Now, therefore, whoever possessed power or sovereignty shall arise in their defence, him God most high shall cause to be victorious in this warfare with these infidels; for he who shall cheerfully expend his wealth, not withholding it in their sacred cause but affording it where required, in order successfully to attack the enemy and drive them forth from the kingdom of Malabar; and, who, further, shall rescue out of their hands the ports of which they have obtained possession, and have brought under subjection to them; he who shall do this shall be called righteous and blessed; as, by the Divine blessing he shall have performed that which it was his duty to do, having alleviated the wounds of his brother in distress, and entitled himself to a reward, glorious, beyond what can be conceived; and, of a recompense which, in its bestowal, shall call forth praise from the people of the East and West, such as it shall not be in their power to give expression to.

Furthermore, this person shall be beloved by and accepted of God and his angels, and the prophet and saints; and for his prosperity the progress of the righteous amongst the servants of God shall avail, and the blessings of the poor and those who are friendless and in distress. Behold, then, how great is the reward of the religious militant, and of him who shall expend his wealth in this, the cause of God, and who shall relieve the distresses of the poor and those in misery. Verily, said the Prophet (on him may be the blessing and peace of God forever rest!), "Whoever shall deliver a believer from any one of the calamities incidental to this life, him will god in turn deliver from some one of the terrors that shall attend the day of resurrection." Now this is a tradition of good authority amongst the faithful. If, therefore, such a recompense shall await him who shall deliver a believer from any worldly calamity, however small, how much greater shall be the future reward of him who shall deliver many who are wretched and forlorn from great and numerous sufferings, by fighting for them, out of piety towards God? Truly, the recompense to this man can be computed by God alone (whose name be forever praised!). For the Lord most high has distinguished the militant against infidelity, and those who set free the friendless and in affliction, in that he hath said, "Wherefore[11] is it that ye do not fight for the true religion of God, and in defence of those among ye who are weak, and for your women and children?" Besides this saying also, there exist many others, and also traditions without number, all showing forth the merit of this holy warfare and of engaging therein, and of expending wealth in resistance to infidels; and regarding the blessings that attend martyrdom. Verily the Lord, Almighty and all Hallowed hath said,[12] "It has been written, that war against infidels is incumbent on you; nevertheless ye are averse to engage in it. Take care, however, that herein ye do not refuse that which is profitable for you, and perchance desire that which shall injure you, for the Lord is omniscient, whilst your understandings are blinded." Further he said,[13] "Surely God has purchased of the faithful their lives and possessions, in that he has vouchsafed up to them the blessings of paradise if they will fight for the cause of God; and whether they kill others or be themselves slain, of this the promises are made sure to them, both by the Tourab,[14] the Injeel,[15] and the Koran. And who shall be more faithful to his covenant than God! Rejoice ye, then, in the Covenant which ye have made, for by it shall ye obtain great happiness." And he said,[16] "Those who expend their wealth in the cause of God and to advance his religion, may be compared to a grain of corn, which produces seven ears, and in each of which are a hundred grains; for God giveth increase where he will, and is all-bounteous and all-wise." And he said,[17] "Consider not those who have been slain in the cause of God as dead, but rather as yet alive in the presence of their God, being filled with joy for that of which, by the grace of God, they have been thought worthy, rejoicing for the sake of those who following, have not hitherto arrived where they themselves are, seeing that both fear and grief are far from them." And it is related in the Soheih of Bukharee and Mossellim[18] upon the authority of Abu-Horeira[19] (of whom may God approve!) that it was once asked the Prophet (upon whom the blessing and peace of God for ever rest!) what act was of all the most meritorious: he answered,[20] "faith in God, and in his prophet"; after this, added he, "fighting in the cause of religion;" and then, "pilgrimage to Mecca." Moreover the same authors, upon the same authority, have written, that the Prophet (upon whom be the blessing and peace of God!) declared, "The Lord has made it incumbent upon him who goes forth in his cause, that he should do so with firm trust in him, and with faith in his prophet. If he shall return in safety he shall be rewarded by the plunder which he shall have acquired; but if shall be slain, then paradise awaits him." Abu-Horeira also has said, "the Prophet declared (on him be peace!), "I swear by him from whom I have derived my being, that there exists not among the faithful one who can reject me, and who shall be found to deny that merit which I have ascribed to fighting for the sake of God; and I swear by him in whose hands are my life, that I not only desire to die in so holy a cause, but that if I possessed three lives, I would cheerfully resign them all in the same manner!" Abu Horeira further says, the Prophet (on whom be peace!) declared, "He who goes forth to contend for God, shall be considered equal in merit to those who practise upon themselves all the austerities and bodily mortifications which have been commanded by God; nor shall the holy warrior be considered to have omitted either prayer or self-discipline whilst he shall be absent in this warfare." Further, on the authority of the same associate, the Prophet (on him be peace!) is declared to have said, "There has no one been wounded in fighting for God but that it is known to God, and who shall not appear on the last day; from whose wound also the blood that flows shall be of a golden hue, and its odour that of "musk,"[21] Anas[22] moreover has related that the Prophet (on him be peace!) declared, "Although to fight in the cause of God is a service of mortal danger, yet of all things in the world it is the best which a man can perform, and shall afford the most satisfaction." Further, said he, the Prophet (on him be peace!) declared, "There is no one who has found admission into paradise, who would desire to return again into the world, except it were that he might find the glorious death of a martyr; for nothing could be an inducement to him to leave the happiness of paradise for this world, unless he could for ten times make surrender of his life for God." Also Jaber[23] (God rest satisfied with him!), relates, that a man said to the Prophet (on him be peace!) on the fatal day of the Ohod,[24] "O thou Prophet! I discern that my death draws nigh, where shall my spirit be?" He answered, "in paradise." On knowing this, the warrior cast from him the dates that were in his hands and rushing into the conflict, fought desperately until he was slain. And Sahal Ben-Saad relates, that the Prophet (on him be peace and blessing!) declared, "To sit astride your horse for one day in contending for God, is a higher satisfaction than all else that the world can afford." Abu Moosa also relates, that one came to the prophet (on whom be the blessing and peace of God!) and asked, "the man who slays to obtain plunder, or he who fights to perpetuate his fame, or he enters the combat in order that he may obtain martyrdom and behold the place prepared for him, which of these three fights most for God, and serves him in the truest way?" He answered, "He who fights in observance of the word of God, he it is who is before all, and he who renders to God the most faithful service," And Abu Saud-ul-Hazree relates, that the Prophet (on him be peace!) declared, "He of all mankind is the most righteous whose faith is sincere, and who freely expends his life and substance in fighting for God." Bukharee also, upon the authority of Abu-Horeira, that the Prophet (on him be peace!) declared, "Verily, in paradise there are a hundred degrees of elevation, and each distinct; and God has promised to those who fight for his sake, the intermediate space between one degree and the other, as the space which exists between the heavens and the earth. When God shall enquire of you then, which degree ye desire, then answer ye, 'Firdoos,'[25] since it is in the centre of paradise, and situated in the most delightful and exalted part of it, above being the throne of the All-merciful, and out of it the rivers of paradise flowing. "Further, Abu-Abas has related, that the Prophet (on him be peace!) declared, "He who shall not arouse himself from slumber, and exert himself in the service of God, him shall the fire of hell receive." And Abu-Kais also says, "I heard Sad relate, that he, with certain Arabs (of whom he was chief) had gone out to fight for God against unbelievers, the Prophet (on whom be peace!) being also of their company; and no food being procurable, except the leaves of trees, one of their party devoured a quantity of these, equal to what a camel or sheep would eat, nevertheless he suffered no harm!" Moreover, Abu Horeira (God rest satisfied with him!) related, that the Prophet (on him be peace!) declared, "He who shall bestow a horse upon one who would enlist himself under the banner of the Most High, and be one who has faith in God and in his promises, surely both the food of that horse and the sustenance of his rider, with the ordure of the former, shall be placed in the scales for his advantage on the day of judgement." Moosellim further relates from that commentator (Abu Horeira), that the Prophet (on him be peace!) declared, "He who shall die without having fought for God, or who never proposed that duty to himself, verily consigns himself to destruction by his hypocrisy." Again, "The infidel, and he who slays him, shall not be gathered in the fire together!" Again, Of mankind he is the most meritorious, who shall urge on his horse when fighting for God; flying forward, as it were, upon his back; disregardless of whatever shall reach his hearing, although hostile; neither being averted by any sound of lamentation that shall assault him, although so terrible, indeed, as to frighten away from him all sense of death and destruction: for neither the man who shall seize upon the plunder of infidels (and whose head shall be almost turned with his good fortune), or he who in the solitude of he desert shall mortify his body by rigid privations and prayer, and so shall have obtained full knowledge of God, shall be compared with him first spoken of although they shall not be without their reward." And Jabir Ben Surmah relates, that the Prophet (on him be peace!) declared, "Verily the true faith shall stand first, and the wearers of the turbans[26] shall fight in defence of it until the last day." Soliman the Persian also relates, that he heard the Prophet (on him be peace!) declare, "To urge forward a horse in this holy warfare for one night and one day, is better than fasting for a whole month, or than the practice of rigid watchfulness during all that time. Now if when so engaged he shall be slain, he has accomplished that for which he lived, and has obtained a provision for himself, being placed beyond the reach of all further "perfidy and trouble." And Akbab Ben Aamir relates: "I heard the Prophet (on him be peace!) when mounted in the pulpit, exclaim, 'O Moslems, promise that only which ye are able to perform, for instance, the exertion of your strenghth and skill in shooting arrows. Your archery it is that I require; your archery only will serve me.'[27]" Further he said: "I heard the Prophet (on him be peace!) declare, "He who learnt the art of archery and afterwards neglected it, is not of our number." Again Abu Masood-ul Ansaree relates, that a man approaching the Prophet with a bridled camel in his hand said to him, "This I devote to the "service of God," whereupon the Prophet exclaimed (on him be peace!), "Unto thee on the day of resurrection shall seven hundred camels be given, all of them bridled."[28]

Musrooh relates, also: "We asked of Abdullah Ben Masood regarding the following saying: ' Ye shall not consider those who have been slain in the cause of God as dead, but rather as yet alive in the presence of their God, enjoying that which has been provided for them.' "[29] He answered, 'We indeed inquired of the Prophet regarding this saying, when he declared to us, - Their spirits are in the belly of the green bird,[30] to enlighten which candles are suspended from the throne of God (by which is implied Paradise), where all desires are fulfilled. Then they (these spirits) shall desire the sights of these candles, when God shall make visible to them his ethereal presence, to the extent of their capacity of discernment. For when God said, 'what desire ye?' they answered, 'what can we desire, we who are placed in paradise, where all our wishes anticipated.' Then god spoke to them after the same manner three times; and when they perceived that he had ceased to address them, they prayed to him, saying: 'O Lord, we desire that our souls may return again to their bodies, in order that we may again surrender up our lives for thy sake.' But He, the Almighty, knowing that this was not necessary for them, ceased to converse with them. "And upon the authority of Abdullah Ben Omar Ben Aas, it is related, that the Prophet (on him be peace!) declared, "In the conflict for the cause of God all earthly things shall perish, save only the true faith." Anas also relates: "I had gone forth with the Prophet (on him be peace!) and with his companions, when he was attacked by the infidel, who furiously attacked him. Then the Prophet (blessing and peace be upon him!) exclaimed: 'Prepare ye to enter paradise, which excels in expanse both the heavens and earth.' The Amir Ben-al-Himam upon this cried out, 'Huzzah, Huzzah!'[31]. The Prophet demanded (on him be peace!) "What meant thou in thus shouting, Huzzah! Huzzah?" He answered: O Prophet, I take God to witness that I so exclaimed, only from the hope that is before me of becoming one of the inhabitants of paradise." The Prophet replied, "Behold! Thou art already "one". He added, "Cast from thee the dates that thou holdest in thy hand, in order that thou mayest partake of those that thou shalt find in paradise."[32] Further the Prophet said, "I also would desire of these dates prepared for me, and which shall give life without end." Al-Himam exclaimed, "Thous hast said truly:" and thereupon throwing from him the dates that he had in his hand, he rushed forward to the combat, slaying all around him, till he himself fell. Further Tirmuzee and Abu Daood have related, upon the authority of Fuzaut-Ben-Abeed, that the Prophet (on him be peace!) exclaimed, "Whenever one shall resign his breath, at that hour his work is finished; except him only who dies when charging the enemies of God, and whose account shall not be closed until the last day, who shall be delivered also from the purgatory of the grave."[33] Again Abu Daood, from Abu-Humamah relates that the prophet (on him be peace!) declared, "He who has not fought for God, has not given of his substance to thou who have, or who has dissuaded anyone of his people from that meritorious work, God has verily cast that person into hell-fire already, not reserving him for the last day." Imam-Ben-Hussain has related also, that the Prophet (on him be peace!) declared, "There shall always remain for me a tribe of my people, who shall fight and slay in the cause of truth, and whose interior shall give evidence of their inward feelings, until that time when they shall last of all destroy the Antichrist."[34] And Tirmuzee relates, upon the authority of Ibn-Abbas, that the Prophet (on him be peace!) declared, "There are two description of eyes, which the fire of hell shall not destroy; the eyes that weep in contemplating the indignation of God, and the eyes which are closed when in the act of combat for the cause of God." Again Abu-Horeira; that one of the associates of the Prophet (on him be peace!) when proceeding to battle, having turned aside into a cave in which were grapes and a limpid stream, exclaimed, "If those who are my companions will excuse me from proceeding with them further, I will take up my dwelling in this cave." On his saying this before the Prophet (on him be peace!) he answered, "Thou shalt not see this, for the merit of all of you who go out to fight for God, is greater than what ye could require, if you were to spend seventy years in offering up prayers in the house of God:[35] for if, indeed, ye desire to be forgiven of God, and to be hereafter admitted into paradise then must ye go forth to fight for God, since he who in his holy warfare shall wound but a she-camel, he is truly deserving of paradise."[36] Further, Abu Tirmuzee and al-Musaee, upon the authority of Abu-Horeira, relate that the prophet (on whom be peace!) declared, "He who falls a martyr experiences none of the pangs of death; except, indeed, it be such sensations as men experience when surprised by joy." And Haram-Ben-Ateek relates, that the Prophet (on him be peace!) declared, "He who shall bestow any of his substance in the cause of God, or for the support of his religion, there shall be written down for him seven hundred fold." And Ibn-Inajib has related it upon the authority of Alee, and Abu Adruda, and Abu Horeira, and Abu-Amamah, and Abdullah-Ben-Omar, and Ben-Abdullah, and Imran Ben-Hoosain (with all whom may God rest satisfied! And who all agree in this account), that the Prophet (on him be peace!) declared, "He who has contributed of his wealth to those who fight for God, and remained at home, for every dirhem that he has so expended, he shall receive seven hundred fold."[37] And after declaring this, he recited the following saying: "For God shall give increase where he will. He who is all beneficent and all wise."[38] And Abu Daood has related upon the authority of Ibn-Abbas (God rest satisfied with him!) that the Prophet (on him be peace!) declared to his associates, "When your brethren were slain on the day of Ohod, God transported their souls into the belly of the green bird,[39] from whence the rivers of paradise flow forth, and where they partake of its fruits, and behold the candles of God suspended in the shadow of his throne. Now when they perceived the purity and sweetness of their food and drink, and the pleasantness of their places of rest, they exclaimed, 'Oh! Where shall we find one who shall carry intelligence to our brethren on earth that we are in paradise, where the practice of mortifications is not required, or the severities of war experienced.' And the Lord, most High, whose name be praised, made answer, 'I will disclose this for your sakes.' Therefore, God most High, revealed that, saying, 'Consider not these as dead who have fallen in the cause of God, but as yet living:' " – besides many other passages of the same import. Further, Hakim relates, from Abu-Moosa Al-Asharee, that the Prophet (on him be peace!) declared – "in the shades of the scimitars is paradise prefigured." And Ibn Majah has narrated it from Anas, that the Prophet (on him be the blessing and the peace of God!) declared, "He who shall resting his life in the cause of God, whatever pollutions he shall have collected about him shall be changed into musk on the last day." Al-Tibranee also has related it (in the Kubeer[40]), on the authority of Ibn Omar, that the Prophet (on him be peace!) declared, "He who shall afflict his head with pain in the name of God, whatever crime was before this lying at his charge, shall now be pardoned." And Waellah relates, that the Prophet (on him be peace!) declared, "Whoever has lost his life in my cause may hereafter contend in the deep."[41] Ad-dilumee also, in his work called the Musnud-al-Firdous,[42] relates, declared, "that to fight for one hour in supporting the religion of God, was better than to make fifty pilgrimages to Mecca." By which he meant to say, that the future reward that shall await the first act shall exceed that awarded to pilgrimage, however many in number. And the cause of the pre-eminence being given to the holy warrior in this, that he truly risks his life and all that he possesses for the sake of God, whilst others also reap the advantage of this self-devotion, which cannot be said of pilgrimages to Mecca, where the benefit extends no further than to the pilgrim himself.

Notes:

1. These are chiefly extracted from the Koran.

2. In the present theology of Muslims, holy duties and religious acts are considered of two kinds, the first being styled kifaya, the second qsr'ayn. The performance of the former (accord ing to dara almhtar) may be deputed another, i.e. to a substitute; but the duties defined by the latter expression admit of no such transfer, to perform then being imperative and indispensable upon every true believer.

3. The right of the Portuguese (who are been alluded to) to settle in Malabar, seems not very consistently questioned by the Sheikh, as his ancestors must have acquired their footing in that part of India by the same kind of invasion as that of which he here complains.

4. The Arabic word *qsr* in a theological sense, implies usually, a certain exemption from prayer. It also means an intervention of three day's journey.

5. In the days of the Prophet, supernatural aid supplied any deficiency in the number of Mahomed's followers, for in his eighth chapter, or the Surah of the Koran, styled "Al-Infal" or "spoils" he would persuade his comrades that they owed their victory at Badr to a thousand angels which were sent by God to his assistance. "When you desired succour from your God and he answered you: Surely I will assist you with a thousand angels." Abulfeda also, in his account of the batte of Badr, says "And God succoured his prophet by his angels."
    Whilst Jellaludeen (the great commentator) would have it, that these angels fought, mounted on pie-bald horses. Other Muslim doctors have greatly magnified their number.

6. Mahomed, after gaining his first victory at Badr (which Abulfeda calls "the greater battle", for Mahomed fought two battles at that place) assumed the privilege of dividing the spoils, and in allusion to which event the eighth chapter of the Koran has its name of "the spoils". The dispute was according to Jellaludeen, between the old men who had not fought but

remained by the standards and the young who had. --- As usual, however, Mahomed made his followers suffer for their credulity, since on ths pretence of haing received a divine commission to distribute all plunder, he shortly after, in his expedition to Al-Nadir, was pleased to assign the whole booty to himself. When dividing the spoils at Badr he was entrusted with a fifth. "For know ye, that whensoever ye shall obtain anything in plunder, a fifth part thereof, shall be set aside for the Lord and the Prophet, and for orphans and the poor, and for travellers." According to Al-beidawai, however, Mahomed, besides these fifths, managed to appropriate on his occasion a scarlet carpet of very rich materials and made of silk. In allusion to the suspicions   of his troops regarding this piece of roguery of his, he thinks it necessary to assure them in his third chapter(or Surah) that a prophet could not be guilty of any act of peculation.

7. The first of these was the great uncle of Mahomed, the second his grandfather. Abulfeda begins his life of Mahomed in these words: "The father of the prophet of God (on whom be the divine blessing and peace) was Abdullah, the son of Abdul-Motaleb."

8. This is according to the opinion of Al-Shafee. The Mahomedan doctors, however, differ greatly in their opinions regarding the division of the spoil.

9. The word amir or emir, literally means " a prince or Lord." It was adopted however as a title by the Caliphs of Baghdad, and subsequently seems to have been used by the descendants of Mahomed through his daughter Fatima, who were the green turban to be distinguished and respected.

10. The Zamorin may be considered to have been the same inveterate foe to the Portuguese that Tipu was to the English. From Maffeius we learn that the Muslims succeeded in exciting suspicion in the Zamorin's mind regarding the objects of Da Gama's visit even, which soon ripened into an enmity towards him and his countrymen, that marked all the subsequent actions of his life, and made him ever ready to assist the attacks of the Muslims upon them.

11. Koran, Soorah al-nisa, or chapter the 4th, entitled "Women",

from its having reference chiefly to their treatment and concerns. According to Al-Beidawi (one of the most luminous of all the commentators upon the Koran), Mahomed here intends to censure those of his followers who had remained behind in Mecca, where the Koreish had detained them, after the Prophet's flight to Medina.

12. Koran, soorah "all-bukur," or chapter 2nd, entitled "The Law."

13. Koran, Soorah "al-toobah", or chapter 9th, entitled "Repentance." In consequence of this chapter being the only one in the Koran to which (bismi-allah) "In the name of God," has not been prefixed, the followers of the prophet regard it with some distrust. As to the cause of this omission the commentators are not agreed, some imagining it never to have been intended to be a separate Surah or chapter, but that it belonged to the preceding one. It is called repentance, in consequence of its commencing with a declaration of immunities, as Mr.Sale translates it.

14. The Pentateuch, or five books of Moses

15. The New Testament

16. Koran, Soorah 'al-bukur,' or the second chapter entitled 'The Cow.' This is the same chapter from which the Sheikh quotes in a preceding page

17. Koran, Soorah "Imran" or chapter the third; a quotation from this chapter occurs in our author's preface. In it Mahomed -- tells his followers that Jesus Christ was taken up into heaven shortly before he was to have suffered death, and that another person upon whom God stamped the likeness of Jesus was seized and crucified.

18. Author of the two traditionary works

19. One of the associates of Mahomed

20. Islam may be considered or divided into two distinct parts. The first Imran, faith, or theory. The second Deen, religious practice. Both these rest on five fundamental points: one relating to "Imran" or faith; the other four to "Deen," or religious practice. The first is the Mussulman's formula "La Ilah illu Illah, Mahomed Rusoolihoo. There is no God but the One God, and Mahomed is his prophet." The others are 1.Prayer and ablutions 2.alms 3.fasting 4.Haj or pilgrimage to Mecca.

21. In these days of degeneracy, it is feared, the Prophet would meet with none sufficiently devoted to accept martyrdom on terms so meagre and unsubstantial as these, that he would here propose to his followers, must be regarded

22. One of Mahomed's associates

23. This person, with all those whose names follow, were of the number of Mahomed's associates

24. To this battle Mahomed makes frequent allusion in the third chapter of the Koran. He lost two of his front teeth in it. According to Abulfeda, the forces of the Koreish were three thousand men, Mahomed's not above one. Besides this disparity "they had only two horses amongst them." The Prophet took one and Abu Barda the other. Shortly the party was terrified by the exclamation of Abu-Ramia (one of the Koreish) "Mahomed is no more." This was too good fortune for the Koreish, however, to be true; Ramia had only displaced two of his front teeth. But in consequence of his archers having gone off somewhat prematurely to secure the plunder, to prevent any after foul play, the prophet was worsted and obliged to fly.

25. Muslims give great many names to Paradise. Besides the above, they call it "Al Jinnet", or the garden; Jinnet Aden, "the garden of Aden;" "the garden of blessings;" each of these according to some, being the appellation of a particular part of the garden, and which all vary in their degrees of felicity. In Firdoos, they say, grows the tree called tobeh or "sweet." According to Mr.Sale, it is supposed to stand in Mahomed's palace, from whence a branch of it is to reach to every true believer's mansion, and which will be laden with pomegranates, grapes, dates, etc. Moreover, like Aladdin's lamp, it will present to him whatever he wishes for, flesh ready-dressed, garments ready-made, horses ready-saddled. The earth of this part of Paradise, according to the Muslim doctors, is to be the finest wheat flour, or the best musk. The rivers which flow from the root of the tree tobeh are to be, some of milk, some of wine, some of honey. The position of garden lastly, is situated above the seven heavens, immediately under the throne of God.

26. The followers of Mahomed

27. This expression is repeated three times in the original Arabic

28. Seven is a favourite number among Muslims also. The first chapter of the Koran to consist only of seven verses. It is entitled Soorah-ul-Fatihah, or "the introductory chapter."

29. This quotation from the Koran will be found to have occurred in a preceding page

30. This is another name only for the garden in paradise called Firdoos

31. Bikhi, bikhi. The expression in Arabic may be viewed as an exclamation expressing ridicule as well as joy. For this reason it was that Mahomed demanded from Himam the meaning of this (as he supposed it) unmannerly interruption. The battle alluded to here, was the defeat of the Prophet at Ohod, spoken of in a preceding page. Abulfeda, in his account of that engagement, says, that on Mahomed's finding himself beginning to be roughly used, he exclaimed, "How shall that people prosper who besmear with blood the face of their Prophet, whilst he would invite them to their God." As the Prophet certainly began the attack, this remonstrance on his part must be thought something unreasonable.

32. Whether the Prophet here alluded only to the dates which, according to him, grew on the tree toubeh, of which some mention had been made in a preceding note, or to his musk beauties, the Hoor-al-uyun, seems doubtful. Probably, however, to the latter, as the food that he proposes for the entertainment of his followers in Paradise consists only of the balam, and the fish hun, and no mention is made of the dates, except when enumerated amongst the various sorts of fruits that the famous tree of paradise was to produce.

33. This is in the Islamic creed of a very fearful nature, for when a man dies, they say his body is visited in the grave by two black and horrid spirits named Nukeer and Munkir which words are derived from the Arabic root "he denied, reproduction,") and who examine him touching his orthodoxy, that is, if he cannot answer "There is no God but the God, and Mahomed is his prophet," they began so to cudgel, belabour, and bastinado him with iron clubs, that his cries are heard (except by those

who remain in the world) throughout the whole universe. They mention also several other kinds of ill-treatment, even worse than this, so that martyrdom must have appeared, compared with what Mahomed threatened his followers if they did not submit to it, in the language of Sancho Pansa, "but mere tarts and cheesecakes."

34. Called in the Arabic Al-museeh-al-dujjal, or the false Messiah. It is the daily prayer of all devout Muslims, that they may never see the day of the Antichrist, dreading through means of the wiles of that impostor the perdition of their souls. Jellaludeen Zamskhshari, and other commentators on the Koran, were of belief that Jesus would hereafter descend from heaven, and having slain the Antichrist, would establish the Muslim religion throughout the world, after which the golden age should begin. How men naturally endowed with good understandings, would have become bewildered with such idiotic vagaries as these, it is not easy to comprehend.

35. The temple or the sacred mosque of Mecca is probably here meant.

36. Considering the value of a she-camel to an Arabian, Mahomed could hardly have pointed out to his followers any more fatal or effectual injury that they could occasion their enemies, than by thus destroying the chief means of their existence.

37. The Sheikh, in making this demand upon the purses of those of his brethren who had rather pay for substitutes than enlist themselves, has been liberal with his authorities for his thus laying them under contribution.

38. This pious exclamation, with others of a similar nature, occurs very frequently through the Koran.

39. Firdoos or Paradise

40. A work similar to the « Soheih » of Bukharee, and composed of tradtions of Mahomed.

41. The allusion in this passage is obscure. The Prophet's meaning probably is, that having thus established his devotion and courage, he is prepared to meet any danger.

42. On "the throne of Firdous," a work written in description of delights of paradise.

Chapter II

Regarding the manner in which the Mahomedan religion was first Propagated in the Kingdom of Malabar

It should be understood that prior to the introduction of Islam into this country, a party of Jews[1] and Christians[2] had found their way to a city of Malabar named Codungaloor,[3] having landed there from a ship of large size, in which they had transported with them also their families and followers. Now the residence of the king of Malabar being in this city, these people petitioned him for the assignment to them of certain tracts of land, and for the grant of certain gardens and buildings; and these by the king's command having been allotted to them, they settled upon them. And some years after this event there arrived at Cranganore a company of poor Muslims, men who had devoted their lives to the exercise of religious austerities, and, who, at this time, under the spiritual guidance of a Sheikh, who was of their party, designed a pilgrimage to the footsteps of our forefather Adam, at Ceylon[4] (on him be peace!) and intelligence of their arrival having reached the King, sending for them into his presence, he manifested towards them much kindness, conversing with them withour reserve: and enquiring of them their circumstances and condition, the Sheikh encouraged by the King's condescension, related to him the history of our Prophet Mahomed (upon whom may the divine favour and blessing forever rest!), explaining also to the monarch the tenets of Islam; whilst, for a confirmation of their truth, he narrated to him the miracle of the division of the moon.[5] Now conviction of the Prophet's divine mission, under the blessing of Almighty God, having followed this relation, the heart of the king became warmed with a holy affection towards Mahomed (on whom be peace!),[6] and, in consequence of this his conversion, he with much earnestness enjoined the Sheikh, after the completion of his pilgrimage to Adam's footstep, to return with his companions to Cranganore, as it was his desire hereafter to unite himself to them; but in communicating, he forbid the Sheikh to divulge this his secret intention to any of the inhabitants of Malabar. Shortly after this the Sheikh with his company sailed in prosecution of their voyage to Ceylon, and from thence, in due time, they retraced their course to Cranganore, when the King instructed the Sheikh to make ready a vessel, and provide it with everything necessary for proceeding on a voyage; directing, however, at the same time, that he should be careful to conceal it from the knowledge of everyone that he was so engaged. Now, there were lying in the harbour of Cranganore at this time a great many vessels, which belonged chiefly to foreigners who were engaged in trade; and the Sheikh, accosting the master of one of them, informed him that it was the desire of himself and his company of pilgrims to embark in his ship: to which the master having consented, when the time for the vessel's departure drew near, the king issued a prohibition to the officers of his household and government from entering into his presence for the space of seven days. He, in this interval of seclusion, selected for each of the several provinces of his dominions an officer to rule over it in his absence, and prepared for the guidance of each of them distinct and detailed instructions, wherein he defined the limits of their several governments; having in view, in this measure, the prevention of any encroachment on the part of any of these his Viceroy's on the territories of another; an event still notorious amongst the Pagans of Malabar: since the sovereignty of this monarch extended throughout the whole of that kingdom, the southern confine of which is Kamhara, and its northern boundary Kanjercote. But to continue our narration – The King, after thus evincing his consideration, embarked with the Sheikh and his poor comrades, proceeding on board the vessel under the concealment of night: and setting sail, they shortly arrived off Fundreeah, where the King landing, remained a day and a night; and again embarking, the ship proceeded on to Durmuftun, where the King, with the companions of his voyage, stayed three days; at the expiration of which time they again set sail, touching no where until they reached the coast of Arabia:[7] here the King and all on board the ship having quitted it, remained for a considerable time. Subsequently, however, having projected to return to Malabar, for the purpose of erecting mosques and disseminating the Mahomedan religion in that country, when about to set out upon their voyage the king fell sick; and his disease proving of a mortal nature, he solemnly enjoined those who had accompanied him from his outset upon the expedition.(and these were Shiriff-Ben-Malik and his brother from Alaim,[8] Malik-Ben-Deenar and his nephew Malik-Ben-Habeeb, Ben Malik and some others) not to abandon their voyage from Malabar, after, or in consequence of his death. But on these replying to him, that they were ignorant both of the position of his dominions and the extent of his sovereignty, and adding, that their attachment to his person was their only inducement for having consented to accompany him, the King became thoughtful and perplexed. After remaining for sometime, however, absorbed in reflection, he wrote for them, in the character and language of Malabar, a description of his territories and kindred, detailing also the names of the different governors who had been appointed by him throughout his dominions. Further, he instructed the persons above named, that they should either proceed to Cranganore, or to Durmuftun, or to Fundreeah, or Quilon; making this his last solemn injuction to them: "But tell ye not to any of my people of Malabar of the violence of my sufferings, or that I am no more:" and after this he surrendered his soul to the unbounded mercy of God. Now, some years after this event, Ebn Malik, and Malik-Ben-Deenar, and Malik-Ben-Habeeb, with the wife and family of the latter, besides others of their relatives and dependants, setting sail in a vessel for Malabar, arrived off Cranganore, and having landed there, they proceeded to deliver the letter of the deceased King to his viceroy at that place, concealing, however, from him the fact of his death. And this chief having informed himself of the nature of the instructions conveyed in this mandate, assigned to the bearers of it certain lands and gardens, as therein directed: and upon these being settled they erected a mosque. Malik-Ben-Deenar resolving to fix himself there for life; but his nephew, Malik-Ben-Habeeb, after a time quitted this place, for the purpose of building mosques throughout Malabar. And with this design he proceeded first to Quilon, carrying with him thither all his worldly substance, and also his wife and some of his children. And after erecting a mosque in that town and settling his wife there, he himself journeyed on to Hubaee Murawee, and from thence to Bangore, Mangalore and Kanjarakote, at all which places he built mosques; after accompanying which, he returned to Hubace Murawee, where he stayed for three months. And from this town he went to Zaraftan and Durmuftun, and Fundreeah, and Chaleeat; in all of these towns also raising mosques, remaining five months at the last place, and from thence returning to his uncle Malik-Ben-Deenar at Cranganore. Here, however, he stayed but a short period, soon again setting out for the mosques that he had erected at the above mentioned towns, for the purpose of consecrating and endowing them; and after doing this, he once more bent his steps towards Cranganore, his heart being full of gratitude towards God, because of the dawning of the light of Islam on a land which teemed with idolatry. More-over, Malik-Ben-Deenar and Malik-Ben-Habeeb, with their associates and dependents, afterwards removed to Quilon, where the latter and his people remained. But Ben-Deenar, with certain of his companions, sailing from thence for the coast of Arabia, on their arrival there, proceeded to visit the tomb of the deceased king. Subsequently, Malik, travelling on to Khorasan, there resigned his breath. As for Ben-Habeeb, after settling some of his children in Quilon, he returned with his wife to Cranganore, where they both exchanged this life for a better. Now, in what I have above related, you have the common and earliest tradition that exists, regarding the propagation of the Mahomedan religion in Malabar. Touching the exact time when this event occurred there is no certain information; but there appears good ground for the supposition that it happened about two hundred years after the flight of the Prophet (A.D.822) (to whom be all blessing and praise ascribed!). Notwithstanding that, amongst the Mahomedans of Malabar, the conversion to Islam of the king (before alluded to) is believed to have taken place in the time of the Prophet (upon whom be blessing and peace!), it having been occasioned by that monarch's perceiving in a vision, during night, the partition of the moon, which miraculous circumstance induced him to act upon a journey to vist the Prophet (upon whom be blessing and peace!), and having been blessed with an interview with him, he returned to the coast of Arabia, designing to return to Malabar with the individuals before named, when he died there. There is, however, but little truth in this account. It is a fact, moreover, now well known to all, that the king was buried at Zafar, instead of on the Arabian coast of the Red Sea, at which place his tomb can be seen by everyone, and is indeed now flocked to on account of its virtues. And the king, of whom this tale is told, is syled by the people of that part of the world, As-Samari, whilst the tradition of his disappearance is very common throughout the population generally of Malabar, whether Moslems or Pagans, although the latter would believe that he has been taken up into heaven, and still continue to expect his descent, on which account they assemble at Cranganore, and keep ready their wooden shoes and water,[9] and on a certain night of the year burn lamps, as a kind of festival, in honour of his memory. Further, it is a prevailing belief amongst these people that the king, when the time of his departure drew nigh, made a division of his kingdom amongst his companions, giving a share to all, except to the chief, who afterwards became the Zamorin, and who at this time had possessed himself of the harbour of Calicut, being absent at the time of this division; and who, when he afterwards appeared in the royal presence, was presented by the king with a sword, saying, "Strike with this, and thou shalt reign;" and having faithfully observed this injuction, before a long season had elapsed, he obtained possession of the city of Calicut, where the Mahomedan emigrants had settled, and whither merchants and men possessed of wealth flocked from various quarters; from these sources its trade increased with such rapidity that the city became greatly enlarged in size and importance, there being congregated in Calicut men of all nations, whether believers or heretics. The increasing authority of the Zamorin, also, amongst the Rays of Malabar and the chieftains of that country (the whole of whom were Portuguese, and possessed of various degrees of authority and power) became manifest, in that, whilst the authorities of some became the prey of others, by means of the assistance and the cooperation of the Zamorin, and through the blessing that attended him from the prayers of the deceased king (who had enjoined him to make conquests), yet notwithstanding, the territories of his dependants remained secure and unmolested: this proceeded from the divine blessing of the Prophet (on whom be peace!) and from the influence of that religion which acknowledges him as its founder. And amongst its chieftains above alluded to, there were some whose territories did not exceed one parasang in extent, while others exercised rule over far more extended domains. Some, again, had at their command only 100 soldiers, whilst others could bring into the field from 200 to 100,000 men and some even more than this last number. It was not unusual however, for certain cities to make a league amongst themselves, two or three together, or sometimes a greater number, having in view in this alliance their general safety; and notwithstanding that one city might be more powerful and could command more men than another, yet when a league of this description had once been entered into, although occasional quarrels and disagreements might occur, the treaty of amity between them was never entirely disregarded. Now amongst those who possessed the greatest number of troops were Juroodee, the Ray of Quilon, and Kumharee, and others whose countries lay between, and to the east of, those towns, and whose territories were of considerable extent. After these came Kolturee, the Ray of Hubbee Murawee, and then the chieftain of Juruftun and Cannanore and Akdad, and Durmuftun, and others of similar extent of territory, all of these being famous for their power and wealth; but the most distinguished of them was the Zamorin, chiefly owing to the blessed influence of the religion of Islam, and resulting from the regard manifested by him for its followers, and from his kind treatment of them generally, but particularly as evinced towards those of them who were strangers and in want. Notwithstanding that, the pagans would have ascribed his ascendancy to the sword presented to him by the king, before alluded to, this sword to this day being in the possession of the Zamorin, preserved by him with great veneration and respect, and carried by him wherever he goes forth to battle or into any great assembly. With regard to the wars of the chieftain, whenever he commenced hostilities against any of the inconsiderable chiefs of Malabar, provoked to do so by any aggression on their part, after subduing them, it was his practice to return to them some portion of their possessions, provided he had not been irritated beyond measure; and this restitution, although sometimes delayed for a long time, he always made in the end, herein evincing a polite regard for the prejudices and feelings of the people of Malabar, who have a great reverence for all old customs and observances, of which this preservation of ancient right formed one which was never broken though, except on some extraordinary occasion; and particularly, as to act in this way was contrary to the natural disposition of the Zamorin, which dictated to him in war nothing but the destruction of lives and desolation of countries, to the utmost extent which it should be in his power to effect.

Notes:

1. The Jews, according to a tradition which exists amongst the body of that nation who reside at Cochin, came to India from Persia, after they had been freed from their servitude by Cyrus, about 540 years before the birth of Christ. Fra Paolina, however, seems to doubt this account of their origin, and Dr.Forster quotes a Portuguese work entitled "Noticias dos Judeas de Cochin," which says, that about A.D.369, seventy or eighty thousand Jews were landed from the kingdom of Majorca, on the Malabar coast.

2. These were the Christians of St.Thomas's Mount, or Nestorians, who, according to Paolina, were partly descended of those original inhabitants of the land who were converted to the Christian faith by the apostle Thomas, and partly of other Christians who went from Mesopotamia and Chaldea to India, and with whom the coast of Malabar abounds.

3. Cranganore. Here the Jews established themelves, founding a small kingdom. The origin of black Jews, Dr.Forster ascribes to the custom of the white one purchasing slaves and converting

them to their religion. These Jews, he says, were so much opposed by the Portuguese that in the year 1565, the body of them at Cranganore were obliged to beg protection from the king of Cochin. It was probably about this period, therefore, that the greater part of the white Jews removed to the latter place, and where they are now chiefly to be found.

4. According to tradition, the Muslims believe that Adam fell from Paradise on the mountain of Serendib or Ceylon, where there is still a mountain which the Portuguese call 'Pico de Adam.' – D'Herbelot. According to the same author, Eve is supposed to have alighted in her fall from Paradise at Jeddah in the Red Sea.

5. This miracle is styled in Arabic Ishfak-ul-kumur, or "the fissure or division of the moon." It is only justice, however to Mahomed to remark, that this miracle, like those of the doves flying to his ear, and the camels addressing him, were not of his own fabrication, but were ascribed to him after his death by his fanatic followers. Mahomed himself was too wise to boast of any miraculous power; indeed in the following and other passages he disclaims it: "Say, I declare not unto you that the tresures of God are at my power, neither do I say unto you verily I am an angel, I follow only that which is revealed unto me." Koran, Surah or Inam, chapter vi, entitled "Cattle."

6. This benediction, in imitation of the Koran, is expressed in the mystical abbreviation of salam, for sul-luh-lah-oo aleihi va sulum, may God bless and preserve him.

7. The word in the Arabic Shuhar, includes the whole line of coast from Oman and Aden.

8. A town in Persia.

9. So that, in case of his descent taking place, he might not want these accommodations. The wooden shoes are peculiar to the Brahmins.

Chapter III

Relating certain peculiar customs that distinguish
The Pagans of Malabar

Now it must not be concealed, that there are found amongst
the pagans of Malabar usage of an extraordinary nature which are
unknown in any quarter of the world; and amongst these may be
instanced the following: Should the Ray, or chieftain of any tribe of
them be slain in battle, his troops continue a war of extermination
against those who were the occasion of his death, attacking them
and their cities, until they have succeeded in annihilating the one
and laid desolate the other. From this cause, therefore, it happens
that their enemies cautiously avoid killing any of their Rays, dreading the consequences which from this ancient custom are
inevitable; although, in latter days, less apprehension is shown by
those opposed to them in this particular. The Rays of Malabar are
of two parties: the first, those who support the Zamorin; the second, those who are in alliance with the Ray of Cochin. Now this
division is only occasioned by the circumstance of the rivalry of
those two great chieftains; and which when it shall be at an end, this
distinction of party will also cease.[1] In their wars they seldom have
recourse to treachery; but fixing upon a certain day with their
enemies when to decide their quarrel by arms, they regard any
treacherous departure from this engagement both as base and
unworthy. Upon the death of any great person or near relative, as a
father or mother, or elder brother, amongst the Brahmans of Malabar
(comprising carpenters and people of that description), of a mother,
or maternal uncle, or elder brother, amongst the Nairs, and their
connections, the men of both these castes will abstain for a whole
year from associating with women and from eating animal food;
during this time, also, neither shaving their hair, nor cutting their

nails, but rigidly enduring these and such mortifications, out of reverence to the memory of the dead. The laws of inheritance amongst the Nairs, and other castes allied to them, make property to descend to the brothers from the mother, and to the children of their sisters and maternal aunty, and to all who are descended from the mother, and not to the immediate offspring. And this peculiarity of excluding the immediate off-spring, has been adopted by the greater part of the Mahomedans of Cannanore and those who are dependent on them in the neighbourhood of that place; although there are not wanting among them, who read the Koran, treasure up its maxims, and study it with apparent zeal, being seemingly desirous to improve themselves by science, and who are regular in the performance of religious worship. Amongst the Brahmans and the trades, such as painters and carpenters, ironsmiths and labourers generally, and amongst fishermen and other castes of a similar description, inheritance goes to the children born in marriage; but amongst the Nairs there is no such ceremony as marriage, a string worn round the neck of a woman being all that gives sign of her marriage; and this only being worn by her when the first forms such connection, for she afterwards throws it off or continues to wear it, as her pleasure or expediency dictates. With regard also to the marriage of the Brahmins, when there are several brothers in one family, the eldest of them alone enters into the conjugal state[2] except in case where it is evident that he will have no issue), the remainder refraining from marriage, in order that theirs may not multiply, to the confusion of inheritance. The younger brother, however, intermarry with women of the Nair caste without entering into any compact with them, thus following the custom of the Nairs, who have themselves no conjugal contract. In the event of any children being born from these connections, they are excluded from the inheritance; but should it appear evident that the elder brother will not have issue, then another brother, the next to him in age, will marry. Among the Nairs and the castes connected with them, two or four men live with one woman[3] each of them in turn passing the night with her, in the same manner as a Mahomedan divides his caresses amongst his wives; and it is seldom that any hostility or disagreement takes place between the men, in consequence of this their possession in common of the same female. The carpenters and ironsmiths, and painters, and others of their description, following them in their custom, cohabit two or more together with one woman, but not unless they are brothers or in some way related, lest confusion should ensue in the inheritance of property. The Nairs have their bodies for the most part exposed, meaning only a covering around their middles. In this custom, both men and women, and kings and nobles, without exception, agree. Neither do they conceal their women from the sight of anyone; for whilst the females from the Brahmin caste are kept veiled from sight, the Nairs adorn their women with jewels and fine clothes, and bring them out into their great assemblies, for the men to behold and admire. Touching the laws of succession to the sovereignty, none but the eldest of the akhuns, or sons of maternal uncles, can succeed; although this first born should be dumb, or besotted in intellect, or blind, or incompetent. Notwithstanding this law, it has never been heard of, that any of the akhuns has ever conspired against anyone of his elder brethren in order to clear the way for his own more speedy accession.[4] In the event of failure of rightful heirs, or of any scarcity of them, they make choice of a stranger (provided to be a person advanced in age) to succeed, instead of the son, or brother, or nephew; and after this adoption they make no distinction between him and a lawful heir. And this custom prevails with all the pagans of Malabar, whether in the succession to the kingdoms and high dignities, or to the most inconsiderable patrimonies; a perpetuity of heirs being thus secured to them. The Nairs are thus subject to troubles without end, which they patiently endure, from their division in castes, countless in number, of high, low and all intermediate degrees: for, if it happen that one of higher shall come in contact with one of inferior caste, or approach him nearer than the distance prescribed for him in his intercourse with inferiors, it becomes necessary that he bathes himself, it being unlawful for him to eat before this ablution, because, should he neglect this participation, he would be degraded from his caste, and could never afterwards be admitted into any but the lowest grade. Indeed, he seldom finds security, except in flying to some place where his degradation, and the cause of it, shall be unknown; otherwise the head magistrate of the district to which he belonged would probably seize him and sell him as a slave to one of an inferior rank, being even indifferent whether his purchaser be a boy or a woman.[5] Sometimes, one thus situated will come over to us, and embrace Islam, or will turn Yogee (or religious mendicant), or Christian.[6] Upon the same principle of jealous restriction, one of high caste cannot partake of food which has been prepared by one of lower grade; for should he do so, he has only the alternative above mentioned. Those who wear the string carrying this badge of caste around their necks, and to whom these restrictions apply, are the highest of the pagans of Malabar. But these, again, are divided into classes, which are both of high, low and all intermediate degrees; the Brahmans, who also are of various grades, ranking above all. After them come the Nairs, who are the soldiers of Malabar, and who are very numerous and possessed of great power: of them also there are different classes, from the highest to the lowest. Then the cultivators and shanars,[7] the occupation of the latter being to climb the coconut trees, gather the fruit, and extract the juice from its branches which becomes a fermented liquor of an intoxicating nature. After these came carpenters, iron-smiths, painters, fishermen, and numerous other classes who are labourers generally: also those whose occupation consists in the cultivation of the ground. Of all these various distinct classes, on any illicit intercourse taking place between a man of inferior caste and a woman of high rank,[8] whilst the intimacy subsists, the woman is degraded from her caste, unless she should bring forth a male: but, should she not become pregnant from this connection, the husband seizes her and sells her as a slave; unless she should fly to us and embrace Islam, or turn Christian, or become a Yogee. In the same manner, should a man of high caste have intercourse with a woman of low caste the former would be degraded, and have no remedy but in one of the alternatives above mentioned. An exception to this rule, however, is made in the case of the wearers of the threads, who have intercourse with Nair women without being subjected to this penalty; this exemption in their favour arising from the law that exists among them with regard to the marriage of the elder brother only, the younger ones being thus driven to connect themselves with Nair women. Further, to how many more troublesome and unmeaning usages of this nature do they foolishly submit themselves, thus multiplying vexations! The mention, however, of their customs that has already been made, would hardly have been consistent with decency, or indeed with justice, had it not appeared indispensable for the true understanding of what follows in these pages: but to return to our relation. Sherif-Ebn-Malik, and Malik-Ben-Deenar, and Hubeeb-Ben-Malik, and their companions, of whom mention has been already made, on their first settling in Malabar, by building mosques in the ports above-mentioned, and disseminating throughout the adjacent country the Mahomedan religion, gradually brought over the inhabitants to Islam, whilst merchants from various parts frequented these ports. The consequence was, that new cities sprang up: and amongst the number of these may be named, first, Calicut, Baleenkot and Travankad; then Tamoor, Timan, and Poorangar; after these Purinoor; and in the neighbourhood of Shalleat, Kabkat, and Turkoree, and other towns around Fundreeah, and Cannanore, and Adhkat, and Travinkar, and Meila and Chumpa; in the vicinity of Durmuftun, also, and to the south of it, Buduftun and Nazoourum and to the south of them, Cranganore and Cochin, and Beit and Balurum, besides other sea-port towns. Now in all these the population became much increased, and the number of buildings enlarged, by means of the trade carried on by the Mahomedans, towards whom the chieftains of these places abstained from all oppression; and, notwithstanding that these rulers and their troops were all pagans, they paid much regard to this prejudices and customs, and avoided any act of aggression on the Mahomedans, except on some extraordinary provocation; this amicable footing being the more remarkable, from the circumstance of the Mahomedans not forming a tenth part of the population. Now, the sea-ports of Malabar, from the earliest times, have possessed importance; amongst the most considerable of which the port of Calicut formerly ranked; though it has now become much diminished in power and wealth, in consequence of the arrival of the Franks in Malabar, and the hindrance offered by them to the trade and commercial pursuits of its inhabitants. The Mahomedans of Malabar, however, having no emir amongst them possessed of sufficient power and authority to govern them, are consequently under the rule of the pagan chieftains, who faithfully guard their interests and decide between them, besides granting to them advantageous privileges; and should any Mahomedan subject himself to the punishment of fine of them, notwithstanding his delinquency, or any other provocation, their treatment to the faithful, as a body, continues kind and respectful, because to them they owe the increase of towns in their country, these having sprung up from the residence of the faithful amongst them, and from their ceremonious observation of Friday and of the festivals, and from their appointing sacred seasons for prayer, and for the due performance of the divine duties amongst them. For the Mahomedans do not permit the profanation of Friday; he who profanes it subjecting himself, in the greater part of the countries of Malabar, to fine and punishment. If a Mahomedan shall have committed a crime mostly of death, and which by the laws of the inhabitants of the country is considered capital, having first obtained the assent of the principal Mahomedans, the pagans put him to death, and after his execution deliver his body over to his brethren; who, having washed it and placed it in a coffin, offer up over it the prayer for the dead, and afterwards give it a burial amongst the dead of their sect: but when a pagan has been condemned to die, having put him to death and gibbeted him, they leave his body to be devoured by dogs and jackals. Regarding the imposts of the chiefs of Malabar, they exact a tenth part upon all articles of merchandize; they levy penalties and deodands, also when anyone has subjected himself to them. Now, they demand no land-tax from the tenants of the lands and gardens, although they are of great extent: they refrain also from entering the houses of the Mahomedans without their permission. On the occasion of a Mahomedan being guilty of any crime, or of injuring the person of another feloniously, the chief of the pagans calls upon his brethren to drive him out from amongst them, and to degrade him and bring him to punishment. Lastly, the Nairs do not protest their countrymen who have abjured idolatry and come over to the Mahomedan religion, nor endeavour to intimidate them by threats, but treat them with the same consideration and respect that they evince towards all other Mahomedans, although the persons who have apostatised be of the lowest grade. In short, in consequence of the friendly treatment that they uniformly experienced from these people, the Mahomedan merchants in ancient times were induced to come amongst, and associate with them.

Notes:

1. According to Paolino, kings of the first rank were the Samuri and Perompadapil (the king of Cochin), who were always at war with each other. To the second rank belonged the kings of Janum, Codangalar, Pupurangari, Airur, Cannanore, Rapolun, Cajamcollam, Parur, etc. Those of the third were called Kartava, i.e. prince or Lords; such were the Karatavas of Panamacatta, Cunateri, Massuanani, etc.

2. Fra Paolino remarks that on the coast of Malabar a custom prevails in the caste to which the braziers belong, that the elder brother alone should marry. This custom is not restricted to the braziers, but extends to the Brahmins and others.

3. This custom, Dr.Forster thinks may perhaps cause more males to be brought into the world, and thus supply the check to population which Fra Paolino is of the opinion takes place in India, from the following causes: 1st The small pox. 2nd. Polygamy. 3rd. Continual wars and revolutions and 4th. The oppression of rulers.

4. Buchanan has remarked that to a European the succession among Malabar chiefs appears very extraordinary.

5. Adultery also was, according to Fra Paolino, punished with this penalty. If a woman was guilty of it, she lost, he says, the prerogative of her caste, and was sold as a slave to some foreigner whether Christian, Jew or Muslim. He adds that this was the case, in particular, with a celebrated wife of a Brahmin at Allangata, who had been degraded and sold, and who was

afterwards baptized by the Bishop of Arcopolis in Malabar.

6. Paolino baptized, he tells us, a Brahmin woman at Edapulli who had been guilty of adultery. "When I asked," said he, "why she wished to embrace the Roman Catholic religion?" she replied, "Inika Dosham vanica poi," that is, I have been guilty of sin." Her explanation would seem to pay but an equivocal kind of compliment to the creed of the good Carmelite father.

7. These are a caste of Malabars whose employment it is to gather betel-leaf, extract toddy, etc.

8. According to Paolino, it was only women of a lower class than the Brahmins that were sold as slaves when they held any criminal intercourse with men of inferior condition for he says, "This crime is overlooked when women, over whom their caste has no power, lead irregular lives, or when they indulge in such licentiousness with men belonging to higher caste."

Chapter IV

Being and Account of the Arrival of the Franks in Malabar, and of their villainous proceedings in that country. And this chapter is divided into Sections

Section I

Relating the first Appearance of the Franks in Malabar, the Occurrence of Hostilities between them and the Zamorin and their building fortifications at Cannanore; also, their seizure and occupation of the Harbour of Goa.

Now, the year in which the Franks first visited Malabar was the 904th of the Hijira,[1] when three of their vessels having, towards the close of the Indian season,[2] anchored off Fundreeah,[3] a party from on board left the ships, and proceeded by land to Calicut. At this city they remained for some months, employing themselves in gathering information of the statistics and condition of the several countries of Malabar;[4] but, on this occasion, they abstained from engaging in trade, and at the expiration of the above period returned to their own country in Europe.[5] And the occasion of this visit of the Franks to Malabar was, according to their own accounts, in quest of pepper lands, they being greatly desirous of establishing a trade in that spice; because, at this time, they could only procure it from those who brought it from the original export-ers of the article from Malabar.[6] And two years after this[7] their first appearance, a second party of Franks arrived[8] in a fleet of six vessels, which, having anchored off Calicut, they landed at that port, and assuming the character of traders began to engage in commerce. But no long time had elapsed before they endeavoured to persuade the agents of the Zamorin to prohibit the Mahomedans from engaging in the trade of the country, and from making voyages to the ports of Arabia, saying to them, "the advantages that you will derive from a commercial intercourse with us will greatly exceed any that they can afford you." In the same spirit also these Franks proceeded to trespass on the property of the Mahomedans, and to oppress their commerce.[9] Now, in consequence of this conduct on the part of the Franks, the Zamorin having resolved upon their destruction, he attacked them and put to death sixty or seventy men of their party, the rest escaping by flying to their vessels, from which they opened a fire upon the people on the shore, who in return commanded them. Shortly after this event they sailed into the harbour of Cochin,[10] and imposing themselves upon its inhabitants as an inoffensive and honest race, they succeeded in building a mud fort[11] at that place which was the first piece of fortification that was constructed by them in India. And after taking up their dwelling in this building, they proceeded to demolish the mosque which stood on the sea-shore at Cochin, erecting in its place a Christian church,[12] whilst they imposed the labour of building this edification upon the inhabitants of Cochin (A.D.1503). Moreover, having ingratiated themselves with the people of Cannanore,[13] these Franks contrived to erect a fort there also, employing the natives of that town in its construction. These fortifications completed, and having laden their vessels with pepper and ginger, they set sail for the countries of Europe, for, as has been before remarked, a commerce in those spices was their chief object in traversing so vast a distance; and at the expiration of the year[14] another party of Franks returned in a fleet of four vessels; and landing as before at Cochin and Cannanore, and taking in pepper and ginger at these ports, they again set sail for their own country. About two years after this a larger party of from eighteen to twenty-two ships[15] arrived at the forts above-named, and having freighted their vessels with spice and such other articles of merchandize as the country afforded, they returned to Europe; in this manner, this commerce became each year more enlarged, and of greater importance. At this time, however, the Zamorin, having resolved to make a descent upon Cochin,[16] proceeded against it, carrying devastation in his course; thus following the usage of war amongst these nations from time immemorial. And in this expedition two or three of the Rays, or principal persons of Cochin, were slain, when, satisfied with his success, the Zamorin returned to Calicut. With regard to the cause of this act of hostility on his part, he was provoked to it in consequence of the Franks having been allowed by the people of Cochin to supplant the Akhuns, having been alerted also to the sovereignty of Cochin[17] with the territories subject to it, in its vicinity, as much to the prejudice of the rights of their fellow-countrymen, as in opposition to all their ancient regulations of sacred and venerable authority, which fixed the line of succession, according to seniority, amongst the chiefs of their own country, and to whom it was confined. The Franks having succeeded in thus supplanting the rightful heirs, by means of their intrigues at Cochin, where they had firmly established their influence, and were uniformly treated by its inhabitants with consideration and respect; whilst on many occasions they had received their support against their enemies, and when oppressed by necessities.[17] These people were also assisted by the inhabitants of Cochin with money, and had a percentage of a tenth upon all their exports assigned to them; from which connection their power became greatly increased. And a year after the arrival of the fleet of about twenty vessels above alluded to, another consisting of ten ships made its appearance, of which number seven had left Europe in that year, whilst the other three had sailed for Malabar, the year before, in company with the larger fleet of twenty ships; but having from some cause been retarded in their passage, they only arrived now in company with the second fleet of seven ships; which last having laden quickly, shortly set out again upon their homeward voyage. But the three vessels, whose passage out had been so delayed, continuing at anchor at Cochin, the Zamorin found a design of seizing upon them; and collected, with their view, an army of nearly one hundred thousand Nairs, together with a larger body of Mahomedans. As he was unable, however, to approach these vessels sufficiently near to attack them by land, his Mahomedan allies having procured from the inhabitants of Fundreeah three dows, sailed out in them to engage the enemy, when some of them (the former) received martyrdom.[18] And on the following day, the people of Fundreeah and Baleenkat embarking in four, and the people of Fundreeah and Calicut in three dows, proceeded to renew the attack upon the ships of the Franks, and the battle between them raged fiercely. Of the Mahomedans, however, none suffered martyrdom on this occasion; indeed, in consequence of the setting in of the rainy season, the engagement was not decisive on either side, and the Zamorin, with all those that had accompanied him, returned to his seat of government (god be praised!) in all safety.[19] As for the Franks, proceeding on the same system, they every year imported from Europe large fleets filled with men and treasure, making their returns in cargoes of pepper and ginger, and the other produce of Malabar. Now it should be known, that after the Franks had established themselves in Cochin and Cannanore, and had settled in those towns, the inhabitants with all their dependents, became subject to these foreigners, engaged in the arts of navigation, and in maritime employment,[20] making voyages of trade under the protection of passes from the Franks; every vessel, however small, being provided with a distinct pass, and this with a view to the general security of all. And upon each of these passes a certain fee was fixed, on the payment of which the pass was delivered to the master of the vessel, when about to proceed on his voyage. Now the Franks, in imposing this toll, caused it to appear that it would prove in its consequences a source of advantage to these people, thus to induce them to submit to it; whilst to enforce its payment, if they fell in with any vessel, in which this their letter of marque, or pass, was not to be found, they would invariably make a seizure both of the ship, its crew, and its cargo! In consequence of this tyrannical conduct, the Zamorin and his subjects and dependents were driven to a system of retaliative warfare, in which that prince expended vast treasures. And from the same cause, both himself and his people becoming straightened and reduced, he sent ambassadors to certain Mahomedan princes to ask their assistance; all of whom however neglected to afford him any, except the sultan of Guzerat, Sultan Mahmood Shah,[21] the father of that excellent monarch Sultan Mozuffur Shah; and Adil Shah,[22] who was the grandfather of Alee-Adil-Shah (upon both of whom may the favour of God forever dwell!), who caused some vessels and grabs to be equipped, but which were eventually found unfit for proceeding to sea. Besides these princes, the sultan of Eygypt, Kansoo,[23] the Phoenician, also evinced a friendly disposition towards the Zamorin, having despatched the emir Hossein, one of his nobles, with some troops and thirteen grabs to assist him; who having reached the port of Diu in Guzerat, sailed thence to the port of Shei-ool.[24] And in company with the emir was king Ayass,[25] the Naib of Diu, when they fell in with and engaged certain vessels of the Franks:[26] capturing the largest of them, and obtaining a complete victory. After this success the emir returned with his fleet of grabs to Diu, in which port he laid up his vessels during the rainy months; and when these were at an end, reinforcement of nearly forty grabs, despatched by the Zamorin, joined Hossein. These vessels however were small, having been collected in the territories of that chief, and wherever they could be found. But the Franks (whom may God Almighty consign to destruction!), when they heard of the emir being at anchor at Diu, made ready for action, and put to sea in a fleet of nearly twenty ships;[27] and sailing for that port and appearing before it, the emir Hossein, with all the grabs in his company, together with those of the Malabarians and king Ayass, instantly sailed out to sea, the emir not waiting to make any preparation for the encounter; and the Franks (the curse of God rest on them!) waited for their attack, chiefly directing their efforts against the grabs of the emir, of which they shortly captured several, the remainder escaping only by flight; whilst these cursed interlopers sailed away victorious! Such being the decree of God most high, and such his will which is indisputable, and against which nothing can avail. As for the emir,[28] he with some of his companions, and the grabs of king Ayass, and the Malabarians, escaped in safety. After this, returning to Egypt, he prevailed upon the Egyptian Campson to furnish for this war against the Franks twenty-two grabs of large size, and completely equipped; and in command over these were placed the emir Soliman of Room, with him being associated also Hossein:[29] and these chiefs sailing first to the fortified port of Jeddah, afterwards proceeded to Kemran,[30] where the emir Hossein engaged himself in making a descent upon Arabia Felix, carrying devastation into that country. But the emir Soliman, designing to proceed to the port of Aden, returned to Jeddah. At this time, however, hostilities broke out between him and Hossein; and in consequence of the attacks of Hossein upon the lives and cities of the Moslems he left that port. But Hossein having been seized by the sultan of Arabia, was by his order drowned in the sea. And shortly after this intelligence reached Jeddah of the occurrence of hostilities between the Egyptian Campson and the sultan Selim Shah of Room;[31] and also of the fatal consequences to the former in his defeat and death, and the seizure of his dominions by sultan Selim Shah (peace to the remains of this unhappy prince,[32] for the Lord is omnipotent!). Now on Thursday, the 22d day of the month of Ramzan,[33] in the year of the Hegira 915 (A.D. 1509), the Franks made a descent upon Calicut,[34] committing great devastation and burning the Jamie[35] mosque, which was built by Nakuz Miscal; and they attacked also the palace of the Zamorin, hoping to obtain possession of it, as that prince was absent, being engaged in war in a distant part of his dominions. But the Nairs that had been left behind in Calicut having united against these invaders, made an assault upon them and succeeded in ejecting them from the palace, killing at the same time nearly five hundred of their party; a great number also were drowned, and the few that escaped were saved by flying on board their vessels;[36] having been entirely defeated in their designs, by the permission of God most high. Now, both before this time and after it, they made various descents upon the dominions of the Zamorin, burning in these attacks in all nearly fifty vessels that were lying near his shores, and confessing martyr-dom upon upwards of seventy of the faithful. And after the same manner they made a descent upon Aden: but its inhabitants made a stout resistance, and God sent succour to the Moslems, abandoning to destruction the Franks, who by his divine permission were put to flight; and their attempt upon the town was entirely frustrated.[37] Now this happened in the time of the emir Ramazan (to whose remains be peace!): and subsequently to the settlement of the Franks at Cochin and Cannanore they had conciliated the inhabitants of Quilon,[38] and had built a fort there; being induced to do this, as great quantities of pepper were procurable at that town, more of that spice being grown there and in its neighbourhood than in any other place.[39] Moreover, the Franks having commenced hostilities against the inhabitants of Goa, captured that place, proceeded to take possession of it. Now this port was one of those that belonged to Adil-Shah (peace to his remains!); notwithstanding this, however, the Franks having seized upon it, made choice of it for their seat of government in India, proceeding to exercise rule over it. But Adil Shah attacking these intruders,[40] repulsed them; he in turn making it a rallying place for Islam. Subsequently the Franks (the curse of God rest on them!) made preparations for a second attack upon Goa, and proceeding against it with a vast armament and assaulting it, they at last captured it. It is said, however, that they bribed over to their interests some of its principal inhabitants, in which case its capture, was not a feat of much difficulty;[41] and the Franks, on thus re-obtaining possession of Goa, hastened to construct around it extensive fortifications of vast height. After this requisition of this place, their power became greatly increased, everyday receiving some accession to it: for the Lord as he wills, so indeed does he bring to pass!

Notes:

1. Maffeius gives us an interesting account of the departure of Vasco de Gama and his comrades from Lisbon on the 7th of July 1497.

2. As the Sheikh, throughtout his work, distinguishes the western monsoon by the term « the days of pain », it is probable that by « the Indian season , « he means those three months in the year

in which the parts of Malabar are annually frequented, viz. from October to April. Hamilton gives the 18th May 1498 as the date of arrival of Vasco de Gama. Faria-y-Souza, who says that de Gama left Lisbon on 8th of July 1497, reached Melinda on the African coast on the 16th of March, and Calicut on 20th July 1498.

3. According to Osorius and others, De Gama first anchored at a place about two leagues from Calicut, which must have been the port here named Fundreeah.

4. A Mahomedan merchant named Mouzaida, who spoke Spanish, is described by the Portuguese historians as having attached himself to De Gama from an admiration of his character, and afforded him the most important services, by giving him a full description of the climate, customs, and productions of Malabar.

5. The jealousy of the Muslims towards the Portuguese thus early evinced itself, for we learn from the historians of the Portuguese nation, that in consequence of their representations, the Zamorin was induced to seize seven of De Gama's party, and persisting in detaining them, the navigator, by way of reprisal, made prisoners of twenty poor fishermen. Faria-y-Souza has not mentioned the exact date of the return of the first expedition to Lisbon. Of one hundred and sixty five who set sail with de Gama from Lisbon, only sixty ever returned. Maffeius tells us that about hundred fell victim to diseases and the fatigues of the voyage; amongst these were Paulo de Gama, the brother of Vasco.

6. By the almost exclusive possession of the commerce of India, the (till then) inconsiderable republic of Venice had obtained an extraordinary influence among the powers of Europe; then the Portuguese made the discovery of that channel by which they eventually wrested from that state their precious traffic and which, in return, they possessed for nearly a century, before the English, at length attracted by their success, became competitors for its profits.

7. The Zamorin appears to have evinced great satisfaction at the return of the Portuguese on this occasion. Faria-y-Souza had erred in stating that Vasco de Gama commanded on this

second occasion, as Maffeius, in mentioning the appointment of Petrus Alvarius Capralis to the command of this expedition, especially states, that it was out of consideration for de Gama's broken health.

8. This is the expedition of Pedro Alvarez de Cabral, which was despatched in consequence of the report given by De Gama and his comrades of the riches of India. He set sail from Portugal in the year 1500, in command of thirteen ships. Of these vessels, however, of which the historian here speaks with so much national pride, half only, from a succession of storms and other misfortunes, were destined to reach India. Maffeius states the number of fighting men on board this fleet as fifteen; Souza at twelve hundred, amongst whom, he says, were eight Franciscan friars. The instructions given to their leader appear very explicit: the latter historian informing us that in substance they are "to begin by preaching, and if that failed, to proceed to the decisions of the sword. Maffeius admits like wise that Cabral was commanded to avenge if the Zamorin should refuse reparation for the wrongs suffered by de Gama.

9. The Portuguese accounts of this matter differ materially from those here given by the Sheikh. That an early and mutual jealousy should have been entertained by the Muslims and the Portuguese of one another is natural; for when was it ever known that one body of intruders could patiently endure the presence of another, or consent to a division of those spoils, which they had before viewed as exclusively their own. Souza and Osorius also made the first aggression to have been on the part of the Muslims of Mecca, who, they say, not only did all in their power to depress the trade of the Portuguese, but, from the time of de Gama's arrival held secret conferences, resolving upon their destruction, it being their anxious desire that not one man might return, so that European nations, from their fate, might be deterred from any further attempts at an intercourse with India.

10. According to Maffeius, in the month of December 1500, they were received by the Rajah (Trimumpara or Parampadapil) with much hospitality, he desiring to conciliate them, and regarding them as valuable allies against the Zamorin, of whose power he was greatly jealous. Osorius mentions that a strong

house in Cochin was allotted by him as a factory for the Portuguese, and a treaty of commerce solemnly concluded.

11. The fort of Cochin, the first erected by the Portuguese in India was built by Albuquerque in 1503. Fra Paolino, in his account of Cochin, says,: "This beautiful city was built by the Portuguese in the tenth year after the arrival of Vasco de Gama at Calicut." This would have been in the 1508; now it is certain, from the accounts of Maffeius and others, that the fort of Cochin (the first erected by the Portuguese in India) was built by Albuquerque in 1503. It is possible that the good Carmelite father dates the building of the fort from the time of the completion of the cathedral, to the profanation of which by peter van Bitter (who turned it into a warehouse for the Dutch East India Company in 1663) he so feelingly alludes.

12. It is probably of this church that Maffeius speaks. Osorius had recorded it of the Portuguese governor above alluded to (Albuquerque), that when dying, he desired the latter part of the Gospel of St.John to be repeatedly read over to him. He died of chagrin and disappointment at the unworthy treatment he had received from his sovereign; his bones were after wards removed to Portugal, in the same spirit in which epitaphs were raised to the memory of Camoens in poverty and want. The fate of Columbus forms another parallel case of Lusitanian gratitude of this posthumous kind.

13. The trade at Cannanore, with Bengal, Arabia, and Sumara, has always been considerable. Fra Paolino suggests an opinion that the sea-robbers mentioned by Pliny, Adrian and Ptolemy, as existing in this part of India, must have been the Malabar pirates (or Malabars as he terms them) who lived about Mount Illi or Delhi. With regard to the manner in which the Portuguese obtained a footing at Cannanore, the Sheikh does not agree with his contemporary Maffeius, who declares they were invited there.

14. Criminals convicted of capital crimes usually formed part of these expeditions.

15. The scrupulous nicety of the Sheikh in regard to number is here shown. The fleet, he says, consisted of from eighteen to twenty-two ships. According to Maffeius and Souza there were twenty

sail. Vasco de Gama again commanded on this expedition which may be considered the fourth expedition by the Portuguese in India.

16. The Rajahs of Cochin and Calicut were (says Fra Paolino) the only two of the chieftains of Malabar who had a right, as a token of their unlimited power, to have carried before them the branch of a coconut tree bound round with a bandage at the lower and quite free at the top. In consequence of this equality of privilege, they were always at enmity with each other, and the Zamorin, from the support which he received from the Mahomedan merchants at Calicut, was, until the arrival of the Portuguese generally victorious.

17. The Sheikh has omitted to remark, however, that the Portuguese, by the timely succour which they afforded to the Rajah of Cochin, had been the instruments of his restoration, having replaced him upon his throne after he had been driven from it by his implacable enemy the Zamorin. For this service he was indebted to Francis Albuquerque, who relieved him after he had been basely deserted by Vincent Lodre. According to the Portuguese historians, when Trimumpara (the king of Cochin) saw the fleet of Albuquerque coming to his relief, he cried out "Portugal, Portugal!" and ran in an ecstasy to the strand. Besides restoring him to the throne, Albuquerque presented him with 10,000 ducats: a masterly piece of policy, considering the situation in which he stood.

18. The Sheikh throughout his history, when he mentions the death of any of his brethren in their attacks against the Portuguese, uses the Arabic word which may be rendered rather as aspiring to martyrdom or as having suffered it. His meaning however is, that they quaffed the sherbet of martyrdom, as his contemporary Ferishta would have expessed it; a fate, of the happiness of which it has been seen he would persuade his brethren, in the first of his three introductory chapters.

19. Throughout the whole of this passage the Sheikh might be charged (if such a charge were not inconsistent with the evident gravity and simplicity of his character) with a disposition to banter his countrymen. For instance, first, the manner in which he mentions the death of those who on the first day of

the engagement received martyrdom; as if he had said, for "their pains!" Then, his remark upon their safety on the second day, when no candidates for it amongst "the faithful" seem to have been found; and, lastly, the grave piece of congratulation that he offers them and their 100,000 comrades upon having escaped with their lives on this occasion! The chances of safety to the allies could not have been very problematical, considering that in this desperate expedition there were a lac of fighting men (for the Nairs should be all this by birth) against three poor merchant men! It is to this attack that Souza must allude when he states, that in the year 1503, the Zamorin attacked the Portuguese at Cochin with fifty thousand men, both by land and sea. According to him however, the Zamorin's fleet on this occasion amounted to eighty vessels of various descriptions, besides fire-ships. Of these last Maffeius also makes mention.

As the Sheikh has stated at double what the Portugeuse historian describes it to have been, his apparent disingenuous ness in suppressing the existence of the fleet (except the few dows in which his poor brethren were so badly treated) will perhaps be overlooked.

20. Maffeius very often makes mention of a "vectigal" (or toll) or customs of freights, exacted from the Muslims; this probably was the hateful imposition alluded to by the Sheikh. According to Osorius, the Portuguese permitted no ship to sail without one of their passports; whilst Faria says that, with a refinement of oppression, the Portuguese would make the Moorish vessels carry their own letters of condemnation, the passport not unfrequently running, "The owner of this ship is a very wicked Moor; I desire the first Portuguese captain to whom this is shewn, may make a prize of her!"

21. The sixth in succession of the kings of Guzerat, and who was succeeded by his son Mozuffur Shah II.

22. Yoosuf Adil-Shah, the founder of the Adil-Shahy dynasty of Bijapoor.

23. From Maffeius we learn also, that the Sultan of Cambia or Gujarat and the Egyptian "Campson" (as he calls him) were induced to furnish the Zamorin with some troops and ships, in consequence of his earnest appeal to them on this occasion.

24. An island lying off the southern extremity of Guzerat. It was obtained possession of by the Portuguese in A.D.1515. It would seem from Maffeius, that the Zamorin did not confine his solicitations to the Muslim princes only.

25. Called by the Portuguese, "mullik (or king) Eiaz."

26. This was the battle in which Don Lorenzo Almeida was slain, his ship having, chiefly from an accident, fallen into the hands of the Turks. --- The death of Almeida, who was the son of the viceroy of Goa (Don Francisco Almeida), added to the loss of his ship, probably occasioned the defeat which the Portuguese suffered on this occasion. According to Souza, their loss in men was also heavy, one hundred and forty having been slain. From that historian also we learn that the Muslim admiral sent a letter of condolence to Almeida's father at Goa; but this piece of generous sympathy does not (if Maffeius says true) appear to have softened the viceroy's desire for revenge. In his harangue also to the fleet (which is a very beautiful specimen of eloquence) he dwells chiefly upon the death of his son. --- he tarnished his revenge by ferociously massacreing all the Turkish prisoners made by him in an action that occurred shortly after, we learn from his own countrymen.

27. Don Francisco Almeida, on his being superseded as viceroy by Alphonso Albuquerque (A.D.1508), set sail from Goa with a fleet of nineteen vessels, having on board sixteen hundred men, designing to attack the Mahomedans. After landing at Diu, he sailed to the port of Diu, where he fell in with the Turkish fleet, and an action ensuing, the Portuguese were victorious. Souza says that "vast numbers of books were found in the captured vessels of the Turks. All the prisoners were put to death. The Naib of Diu having sent one of his nobles to congratulate the Portuguese on his victory, a truce was in consequence concluded with him, the captures "cannon being delivered over to the king of Gujarat." The loss of the Portuguese seems to have been very small, as Maffeius says.

28. If Maffeius tells true, his flight was somewhat inglorious.

29. Why they could not have been one and the same person however, which the translator is inclined to imagine was the case, the learned historian has not told us.

30. A port in the Arabian Gulf.

31. This prince is called by Maffeius "Selymus Ottomanus Turcarum Imperator."

32. The Sheikh in this and other places makes use of the mystical way of writing so often found in the Koran, employing only the initials of his words, in the manner in which the 2d chapter of the Koran begins; ALM, which is supposed to stand for "Allah Lateef Mujeed." God is gracious and glorious.

33. This was the unfortunate expedition of Fernando Constino, who was slain on the occasion. It seems from the first to have been a most rash attempt.

34. As the months in the Arabic calendar are lunar, in a few years each makes the revolution of the four seasons.

35. The principal mosque in which the Friday's 'Khotbah' or homily is read.

36. The Sheikh it seems must be distrusted in his list of killed and wounded. Maffeius no doubt has considered the wounded as dead men. Souza also states the number of Portuguese who were slain on this occasion at about eighty. Amongst the wounded, he says, was Alphonso Albuquerque. January 1510, he gives as the date of this unfortunate attack.

37. This was probably the unsuccessful attack of Albuqucrque (A.D.1511). Aden was taken however not long after by the Portuguese, by stratagem.

38. It was at this place that Alexis Menezes, the first Archbishop of Goa, opened his conference with the Christians of St.Thomas, compelling them to renounce the doctrines of Nestorians and to enter the pale of the Romish Church. Dr. Forster, regarding this forced union, justly says, "It is a real and lasting monument of shame for the Romish church." An account of the violent measures, as well as acts, used by the Romish church to make the Nestorians unite themselves to it, is to be found in La Croze's work on the state of Christianity in India. It is when speaking of a temple near Quilon, where the eyes of our good Carmelite friar had been justly offended by some vile orgies that were carried on before him, for a participation in which he had got some Christian fishermen a severe beating before the Church

door, as a warning to other Christians not to participate in such abominations in future, that his German translator, Dr.Forster, has the following reflection, in which severity and humour are happily combined: "This conduct of Fra Paolino seems rather unevangelical and harsh, and to have been somewhat in the style of Boanerges, or those sons of thunder, who wished to call down fire immediately from heaven. Our zealous monk procured full power from the magistrate in order to execute his inquisitorial sentence; this no doubt cost him a considerable amount of money, and must have been charged under the head of secret service. Instead of advice and admonition the monk administered a sound beating; this may be properly called obeying the command 'compelle illos intrace.' The other means by which the Indians are converted to the Catholic religion are no doubt of the same kind as this church discipline.

39. Quilon was formerly one of the most considerable places on the Malabar Coast; but since the digging of the canal at Aleppi, that place had become the greater pepper mart.

40. In the year 915 the Christians surprised the town of Goa, and put to death the governor, with many Mussalmans. Upon intelligence of this, Yoosuf Adil Sah with 3000 chosen men (part Dekkanies and part foreigners) marched with such expedition that he came upon the Europeans unawares, retook the fort, and put many to death, but some made their escape in their ships out to sea (Ferishta). Albuquerque first took Goa in Februrary 1510, in which according to Souza, were found vast quantities of cannon and military stores. In May in the same year it was retaken after a siege of twenty days; but a reinforcement of thirteen ships arriving from Europe, he again proceeded against it and recaptured it. – Adil-Shah here men tioned was the grandfather of Alee Adil-Shah.

41. Kummal Khan, regent during the minority of Ismael Adil Shah, made peace with the Europeans (who after the return of Adil Shah to Bijapur had again besiged Goa, and regained it by giving large bribes to the governor), consenting to their retention of Goa on condition of their remaining contented with the island alone, and not molesting the neighbouring towns and districts (Ferishta). Maffeius' accounts agrees with the above,

except that he ascribes the recapture of the place to the gallantry and generalship of Albuquerque, neither he nor Souza having any mention of any bribes being given on the occasion. As the force of the Portuguese amounted to twenty-three vessels and 1500 soldiers, besides the fleet of Madhoo Row, the admiral of Timoja, who assisted at its capture, it is not likely that treachery was necessary, or the Portuguese might be believed to have had recourse to it.

Section II

Recounting some of the wicked acts of which the Franks were guilty

I would have it understood, that the Mahomedans of Malabar formerly lived in great comfort and tranquillity, in consequence of their abstaining from exercising any oppression towards the people of the country; as well as from the consideration which they invariably evinced for the ancient usages of the population of Malabar, and from the unrestricted intercourse of kindness which they preserved with them. Subsequently, however, they were guilty of ingratitude towards God, forgetting the blessings that they enjoyed; going astray, and becoming divided into schisms. On this account, therefore, did God bring down upon them the people of Europe, the Franks, Christians by religion (whom may Almighty God confound!), who began to oppress the Mahomedans, and to bring ruin amongst them; being guilty of actions the most diabolical and infamous, such indeed as are beyond the power of description:[1] they having made the Mahomedans to be a jest and laughing stock; displaying towards them the greatest contempt; employing them to draw water from the wells, and in other menial employments; hindering them on their journeys, particularly when proceeding on pilgrimage to Mecca;[2] destroying their property; burning their dwellings and mosques; seizing their ships; defacing and treading under foot their archives and writings; burning their records; profaning the sanctuaries of their mosques; ever striving to make the professors of Islam apostates from their creed, and worshippers of their crucifixes, and seeking, by bribes of money, to induce them to this apostasy. Moreover, decking out their women with jewels and fine clothing, in order to lead away and entice after them the women of the Mahomedans; slaying also the pilgrims to Mecca and all who embraced Islam, and practising upon them all kinds of cruelties,[3] openly uttering execrations upon the Prophet of God (upon whom may the divine favour and grace ever rest!), confining his followers, and incarcerating them. Further, binding them with ponderous shackles, and exposing them in the markets for sale, after the manner that slaves are sold; and when so exposed, torturing them with all sorts of painful inflictions, in order to exact more from them for their freedom. Huddling them together into a dark,[4] noisome and horrible building; and, when performing the ablutions directed by their law, beating them with slippers;[5] torturing them with fire; selling and making slaves of some, and harassing others with disgusting employments: in short, in their whole treatment of the Mahomedans, they proved themselves to be devoid of all comparison! In addition to this system of persecution, also, these Franks sallying forth in the directions of Guzerat, the Conkan, and Malabar, and towards the coast of Arabia, would there lie in wait for the purpose of intercepting vessels: in this way, they iniquitously acquired vast wealth and made numerous prisoners. For, how many women of noble birth, thus made captive, did they not incarcerate, afterwards violating their persons, for the production of Christian children, who were brought up enemies to the religion of God (Islam), and taught to oppress its professors! How many noble Seids, too, and learned and worthy men, did they not imprison and persecute even unto death! How many Moslems, both men and women, did they not compel to embrace Christianity! And how many acts of this kind atrocious and wicked, the enumeration of which would require volumes, did they not commit! May the all gracious and merciful God consign them to eternal destruction! For sorely did they oppress the faithful, striving all of them, the great and powerful, and both the old and young, to eradicate the Mahomedan religion, and to bring over its followers to Christianity[6] (may God ever defend us from such a calamity). Notwithstanding all this, however, they preserved an outward show of peace towards the Mahomedans, in consequence of their being compelled to dwell among them; since the chief part of the population of the sea-ports consisted of Mahomedans. Now, as it has been before related, when the Franks, on their first arrival, beheld the Mahomedans dwelling at Cochin, and observed their condition in that place; how that, up to that time, they had in no way altered in appearance or at all swerved from their former religious faith and customs, they would have sought to extinguish the light of God by their calumnious insinuations. But it will never be permitted by the Almighty, that infidels should obscure the rays of divine truth. For when their chieftain, haranguing the Ray of Cochin, said to him, "Drive forth the Mahomedans from Cochin, for the advantage that you derive from them is inconsiderable, compared to what you will obtain from an intercourse with us;" he answered him: "These have been our subjects for a length of time, and has contributed to the building of our city; here, therefore, is it possible that we should now eject them?" Lastly, it is worthy of remark, that the Franks entertain antipathy and hatred only towards Mahomedans, and to their creed alone; evincing no dislike towards the Nairs, and other Pagans of a similar description.[7]

Notes:

1. That the Portuguese were guilty of the greatest excesses their own historians admit. Fra Paolino alludes to a work entitled 'Istoria della Vita e Fatti illustri del ven. Monsign. Giuseppe di S.Maria di Sebastini," (Roma, 1719), in which he says these excesses are particularly described. Whilst the Carmelite father, however, admits his own nation's guilt in this matter, he would not have it supposed that he acquits others in an equal degree, for he has the following severe reflection: "Avarice, insolence, dishonesty, infidelity, and injustice will always bring kingdoms and states for destruction; and if there be any truth in this observation, some other colonies, perhaps will not long remain in the hands of Europeans;" as a little before this he speaks with horror of an unmarried Dutch tobacconist at Cochin who kept a whole dozen of females, and yet asserted that it was improper in the Roman Catholic clergy, not to marry. It is probable that his insinuation was chiefly intended against

the Dutch; at the same time that he also, meant it, in a modified degree, for the Protestant English.

2. Maffeius confirms this charge against the Portuguese. Souza mentions that De Gama's having fallen in with a large ship belonging to the sultan of Egypt, on board of which were two hundred and eighty persons, chiefly pilgrims to Mecca. As they refused, he says, to allow the Portuguese fleet to take possession of the vessel, and made a desperate resistance, every person on board was put to death, twenty children only having been spared who were afterwards baptized.

3. M.Dellon, in his account of the Inquisition of Goa, details a system of atrocities practised by that institution, which make's the reader's heart boil with indignation against the nation and government that could uphold so diabolical an establishment. The Inquisition was established at Goa about 1500 A.D., by Don Constantine de Braganza.

4. Of the prison of the Ordinary, i.e. of the Archbishop of God (called by the Portuguese "algovar" and which was used as a Bridewell to the Holy Inquisition, M.Dellon (who was its victim) says: - "This prison was more foul, dark, and horrible than anyone I had seen, and I doubt whether there can be one so nauseaous and appaling." – Whilst immured within it, this author was informed that, some years before, about fifty Malabar pirates having been taken and thrown into this prison, the horrible famine which they suffered induced forty of their number to strangle themselves with the linen of their turbans.

5. To a Mahomedan, the most degrading species of chastisement.

6. Although the Sheikh has not told us so, still it is certain that the Mahomedans of Malabar, were, after all, the first aggressors. For, before the arrival of the Portuguese in India, Fra Paolina tells us that the Nestorians or the Christians of St.Thomas had observed, to their great sorrow, that their mortal enemies the Arabs were always acquiring more influence, and that they were gradually endeavouring to get the chief power into their hands, on which account (and from the persecutions that they suffered from them), they retired from Canara and various other provinces belonging to the Zamorin, and established themselves in the territories of the king of Cochin. They were also

driven to choose from among their number a king, who was called "Belaite" and who was obliged to engage that he would defend them from the Muslims as well as the Hindus. – The barefooted father, however, appears to regard these Nestorians almost in the same light as the Hindus. He describes their Cattanars or priests as ignorant and proud, and as living like irrational animals. Of one of them he tells the following anecdote, which he gives as a specimen of their morality: - "The Christians of St.Thomas are accustomed to abstain from their wives during lent; a certain female Christian having asked her Cattanar, why this custom had been introduced, the priest replied: - "That it was established by the church in order that the wives of the Christians during the above period, might sleep with the Cattanars." There is a little monkish wickedness in this story, probably, but whoever has passed any time amongst the Cattanars of Malabar will hardly believe it destitute of all truth.

7. Here the Sheikh states what was not the case, since of the victims of Auto-da-fés at Goa the greater part, according to M.Dellon, were usually Hindoos. That the hatred of the Portuguese towards the Mahomedans was more inveterate than towards any other class of people is true; and it was so chiefly because they found in them the most obstinate and formidable opponents.

Section III

Regarding the Treaty entered into between the
Zamorin and the Franks. Giving an account, also,
of the construction, by the latter, of a fort at Calicut.

Now, in consequence of the length of time during which
hostilities had been carried on between Franks and the Zamorin,
the treasures and resources of that chieftain became entirely
exhausted, and the Mahomedans reduced to the last extremity, upon
the death of that chieftain, his successor resolved upon peace with
the Franks.[1] And he was chiefly induced to this from the desire that
his Mahomedan subjects should enjoy the same freedom of trade
that the people of Cochin and Cananore possessed, and so recover from the poverty and decay into which they had fallen. For
this and other reasons, then, he entered into a treaty with the Franks,
by which he consented to their erecting a fort in Calicut on the
condition that his subjects should be at liberty to navigate four
vessels every year to the Arabian continent, and to the ports of
Jeddah and Aden. This pacification concluded, these vagabonds,
on the one hand, set about building their fortifications, constructing
them with great solidity; whilst the subjects of the Zamorin, on the
other, made their preparations for despatching four ships to the
Arabian coast (these being laden with pepper and ginger), and
commenced trading to Guzerat and other foreign ports, carrying
with them passes from the Franks, as the trader of other states did,
viz., the people of Cannanore and Cochin; and this accommodation took place in the year of the Hijra 920 or 921 (A.D.1514-15).
On the return, however, to Calicut of the first four ships from their
voyage to Arabia, the Franks, having in this interval completed their
fortifications, forbade the subjects of the Zamorin from further trading
to the Arabian continent, prohibiting also their exporting either pep-

per or ginger; in this manner seeking to secure for themselves a monopoly of this trade; and so rigidly enforcing their embargo upon it, that if any even the smallest quantity of either of the above – named spices was discovered in any vessels but their own, they made seizure of them, and condemned their cargoes.[2] Notwithstanding this aggravated tyranny and oppression towards the Mahomedans and others, the Zamorin[3] continued true to the treaty he had made with them, chiefly from a dread of their evil practices. Secretely, however, the Mahomedans despatched messengers to the several neighbouring princes, endeavouring to engage them to unite with them in hostilities against the Franks, but without success; since it was not so willed by God most High.[4] But may the displeasure of the Almighty descend on those treacherous and deceitful people, who, being informed of this circumstance, conspired against the Mahomedans, and betrayed the secret to their enemies in this time of need and of great peril. And when this attempt of the Mahomedans became known, the Franks attacked them furiously; all of them being actuated by the same spirit, and obeying to the letter, the order[5] of their superiors, notwithstanding the distance by which they were removed from their government; for although dissensions might arise amongst them, yet it was never heard that any one of them ever fell a martyr to his exercise of the authority invested in him. This general obedience to authority enabled them, notwithstanding the smallness of their numbers, to overcome the native princes of Malabar, who, as well as the Mahomedans, were all intriguing for power amongst themselves, every man being desirous of authority, and prepared to encompass the death of all who stood in his way to it. Some time after these cursed Franks had established themselves in Calicut, and settled there, they invited the Zamorin to a house within their fort,[6] under the pretext of presenting him with certain valuable gifts, said by them to have been sent for his acceptance by the viceroy of the Europeans: but their real intention was the seizure of this person. The Zamorin, however, seeing through this stratagem, by means of a sign made to him by a certain Frank, and by the decree of that Providence which over-rules mankind, escaped from amongst them, and was delivered out of their snares by the will of god most High; and, in consequence of his escape, the Franks expelled from their society him of their number, who, in saving the Zamorin, had betrayed their purpose, banishing him, with all his relations to Cannanore. Subsequently to this, in the month of Mohurrum, in the year 923 (A.D.1517), the Franks sailed out from Goa with a vast armament, consisting of a fleet of twenty-eight vessels; which expedition was designed against the fortified port of Jeddah, of which they were desirous to possess themselves; and entering that port, they threw the Mahomedans inhabiting it into a vast panic and confusion.[7] It happened, however, that the Emir Soliman, of Room, was there at that time, having with him two hundred soldiers, and the grabs which the Egyptian (Campson) had navigated to the Malabar coast, for the purpose of being employed against the Franks, but which he had left there; and the inhabitants opening a heavy fire upon the fleet of the Franks, and some of the ships of the latter suffered severely; these having slipped their cables, hoisted all sail, and, steering without the range of the fire from the batteries, sheered off.[8] But the Emir Soliman despatched some vessels in pursuit of them, when it was discovered that they had in their fleet sunbooks,[9] each manned with thirty men. Moreover they took in Kemran, a small galliot belonging to the Franks, on board of which were twelve Christians,[10] whom they brought back with them to Jeddah: after this, these vagabonds steering for Kemran, remained there till the cessation of the western monsoon, when they returned to Goa, entirely frustrated in their designs. This by the Divine permission and the mercy of God!

Notes:

1. The Zamorin appears himself to have made peace with the Portuguese.

2. Pepper and cardamoms, according to Fra Paolina, have always belonged to the royal revenues, and no private person was allowed to trade in these articles. Formerly (he says) those who smuggled them out of the country had their noses and ears cut off; but at present (about sixty years ago) they are only punished with imprisonment. The Sheikh suppresses the mention of all

barbarity emanating from his countrymen and their Pagan allies, probably with the view of placing the undoubted tyranny of the Portuguese in a stronger light.

3. This was the second Zamorin, who is called by Maffeius, the nephew of the deceased Rajah and was according to him, the nephew of the deceased Rajah.

4. The Mahomedan princes of Bijapoor, Ahmednuggur, and Golconda were about this time engaged in their expedition against Ram Raj of Bejanuggur; but, from the rare allusion even by Ferishta to the Portuguese, it may be presumed that in the days in which he wrote, their proceedings did not generally engage much of the attention of these courts.

5. Which invariably directed the extermination of "the Saracens."

6. Of this intended piece of perfidy the translator has not been able to find any mention in any Portuguese author.

7. It is but seldom that our author, where "the Faithful" are concerned, will make so great (and apparently so just) and admission as the above, the prowess of his brethren being with him a favourite theme.

8. This failure Maffeius ascribes partly to the incompetency and delays of the Praetor in command, and partly to the sickness which broke out in his fleet, and which in part obliged him to abandon the enterprise.

9. A kind of Asiatic vessel resembling a galley.

10. The Sheikh here underrates the number. Maffeius calls the vessel captured "lembus unus," which would degrade the Sheikh's galliot into a fishing smack. The prisoners according to the above historian, were sent by Suleyman to his master Selim Shah.

Section IV

Relating the occasion of the hostilities which ensued between the
Zamorin and the Franks,
and the capture of the Fort of Calicut.

Know, then, that the tyrannical and oppressive conduct of
the Franks in Calicut every day becoming more insupportable
(although the Zamorin was compelled to shut his eyes towards it,
as he was unable to suppress it), a disturbance took place
between them and some of the Mahomedans of Fundreeah, who
at that time were at Calicut, and this happened on the tenth day of
Mohurrum, in the year 931 (A.D.1524): upon which occurrence,
the treaty being considered as at end, war and hostilities
recommenced. Before this event, however certain of the inhabitants of Fundreeah, Chumpanah, and of Travancore and
Parpoorangore, and other places, having sailed out in small grabs
and lain concealed, had seized some of the smaller vessels of the
Franks that were engaged in trade, and captures, in all, about ten
of them; this happened in the year 930 (A.D.1523), and prior
thereto. A disagreement also, had occurred between the
Mahomedans at Cranganore and the Jews inhabiting that place;
and a Mussalman, having in consequence fallen a victim, a general
battle took place between them; and the Mahomedans sent
messengers to all their brethren in the neighbouring towns, begging
their assistance, in order that they might make retaliation upon the
Jews. On this appeal, the Mahomedan population of Calicut and
Fundreeah (with the natives of that place themselves) and of their
dependent villages, and of Kabkat, Turkoz, and Shaleeat (with the
natives of Shaleeat), and Purpoorangore, and Travancore, and
Tanoor, and Parinoor, and Tunan, and Baleenghat (which is in the

collectorate of Shaleeat), having all leagues together, prepared to attack the Jews of Cranganore; designing at the same time to extirpate the Franks, and resolved to make no terms with them. And they entered into this combination with the permission of the Zamorin and his entire approbation. This happened in the year 931 (A.D.1524); and the people of the towns above named embarked in their fleet of grabs (which consisted of a hundred sail), commenced hostilities against Cranganore, where they put to death a great number of Jews, and drove out the rest to a village in the neighbourhood of Cranganore, that lies to the eastward of it. The Muhammadans burnt their houses and synagogues, and proceeded to destroy the houses and churches of the Christians[1] of that place; upon which a misunderstanding took place between the Mahomedans and the Nairs residing there, and several of the castes were slain; in consequence of which the Mahomedans who dwelt in Cranganore were compelled to seek for safety elsewhere, and to remove to other towns. In this year, also, the Mahomedans of Durmaftun (with the native inhabitants of that place), and Azgar and Cannanore, and Travancore, and Meilee, and Chumpanah, entered into a league against the Franks, and made war upon them in the same manner as their brethren of other towns had done before. At this time, too, certain of the principal Mahomedan inhabitants of Cochin (men of great learning in the law) distinguished themselves by their activity in war against the Franks; and amongst these were Ahmud-Murkur, and their maternal uncle Mahomed-Alee-Murkar, with their dependents, all of whom, quitting Cochin, removed to Calicut. Now from this and other circumstances, the Franks, (whom may God confound!) having become well assured of the inveterate hostility entertained towards them by the great body of the Mahomedans and the Zamorin, set sail from Cochin with a vast armament, and proceeded to make a descent upon Funan, where they landed early in the morning of the third Sabbath of the month of Jumadee-al-awal in the above year (A.D.1524); and they burnt and demolished the greater part of the dwelling houses and shops of that place, besides certain mosques; cut down, also, most of the coconut tress that were growing on the banks of the river there, whilst great was the number of those who suffered martyrdom. Thus the Franks, quitting the place during the third night after their arrival, proceeded to Fundreeah, where they made a seizure of forty grabs belonging to its inhabitants; and here also martyrdom was the lot of many. Now at the time when the fracas took place in Calicut between the Franks and certain of the Mahomedans of Fundreeah, and in consequence of which the Zamorin had resolved to attack the former, he himself was absent from Calicut, being engaged in carrying on war against certain other enemies of his at some distance; at this time, therefore, he was content with despatching the prime minister, who was called Baleez, against the Franks, with instructions to attack them. Thus commissioned, this person began to act against them with great vigour, taking his measures with prudence, and collecting together the Mahomedans and the Nair soldiers of the Zamorin; the former flocking to his standard (to fight for their religion and cause of God) from various towns and the Zamorin himself setting out for Calicut, and the provisions of the Franks, at this time being expended, they did not await his approach, but evacuated their fort,[2] and embarked all that it contained on board their ships; to facilitate their doing this they made an opening in the wall from within the fort, and in a part which was not visible to those who were without, and abandoning the fort, they set sail in the ships and went away,[3] which event happened on the 16th May of Mohurrum, in the year 932 (A.D.1525). And there were slain, from the commencement of the war up to the victory of the Nairs, of the Zamorins and soldiers, officers, and of the Mahomedans, upwards of a thousand persons! Nevertheless, the rage of the Franks increased ten-fold, whilst their animosity towards the Mahomedans were heightened to the last degree from this capture of their fort; and in this posture affairs had remained for a long period, when the Mahomedans, notwithstanding all that they had suffered in their wars against the Franks, again fitted out small grabs and recommenced trading; sailing to Guzerat and other parts, carrying, however, no passes from the Franks, but being prepared for resistance; and they commenced also exporting, for the above markets, pepper, ginger, and other articles of trade. Although some of these consignments reached their destination in safety, yet the greater part of them either fell into the hands of the Franks or were lost at sea through their instrumentality, and beholding this, the people of Durmuftun and their followers and dependents, towards the close of this season, entered into a treaty of peace with the Franks, and again sailed under the protection of their passes, as they had done before during their armistice, with that nation. But the subjects of the Zamorin, and those connected with them, long persevered in carrying on hostilities against these their foreign enemy; indeed, till they had exhausted their resources, and had arrived at a state of greatest poverty.[4] And in the year 935 (A.D.1528), a ship belonging to the Franks was wrecked off Tanoor, in consequence of the violent and sudden setting in of the rainy season. Now the Ray of that place affording aid to the crew, the Zamorin sent a messenger to him demanding of him the surrender of the Franks who composed it, together with such parts of the cargo of the ship as had been saved; but that chieftain having refused compliance with this demand, a treaty of peace was entered into by the Franks with him;[5] and from this time the subjects of the Ray of Tanoor traded under the protection of the passes of the Franks to erect fortifications on the north side of the river at Funan, upon certain land which belonged to him there. Now the Franks, in the construction of works here, had chiefly in view the molestation of the Zamorin, the plundering of travellers who pass that way, and the laying waste of Funan. And designing to commence the building of this fort, they sailed out of Cochin in a large and well-equipped fleet of galliots, as materials for the work; but when arrived off Funan, by the gracious interposition of Providence, there arose a violent storm of wind, which occasioned the loss of their whole fleet, not one even of their smallest galliots having escaped; and the whole of their crews (composed of Franks and their servants all dependents) perished, the greater number having been drowned, whilst those who escaped the waves and reached the land were slain by the Mahomedans. Large quantities of woollen clothes were obtained from the wrecks of these vessels; but besides these there was nothing saved. In this manner did the Zamorin obtain over them a signal victory; and there did God frustrate the designs of the Franks and their allies, out of his grace and divine favour.[6] Subsequently, in the year 937 and 938 (A.D.1530-31), some of the subjects of the Zamorin and others, amongst whom were Allee-Ibrahim-Murkar, and his nephew Kutti-Ibrahim-Murkar, and other persons of distinction, set sail in a fleet of thirty grabs for Guzerat, the object of this voyage being generally trade, and the greater part of them steered for the ports of Tojarce and Surat, whilst a few of them proceeded to Bassorah: when the Franks, on being apprised of it, equipped an armament of galliots and other vessels to attack them; and sailing into the rivers at Tojorace and Surat, they seized everything that was lying there, capturing every grab and making prize of every thing found on board; but the vessels lying at anchor at Basorah escaped their hands. Prior to this date, also, there had fallen into their possession a large number of grabs that were employed in the service of Sultan Bahadur-Shah of Guzerat, whom may God (because of his holy resistance to these infidels) hereafter greatly reward! A great many grabs, also, belonging to the people of Malabar, had at different times been captured by them; all this happened according to the decree of God, and from his omnipotent will. Nevertheless to God, and towards Him alone, do I look in hope![7] Now, from the causes above related, the power of the Mahomedans suffered greatly, whilst their circumstances became impoverished to the last degree.

Notes:

1. The Nestorians of whom something had been said before, according to Dr.Forster, received their religious notions, customs and expressions from the Syro Nestorian Christians at Baghdad and Bassorah. Fra Paolino has given a very interesting account on them. When he was amongst them (about sixty years ago), they still celebrated their Agapae or love feasts, as was usual in former times, and which Dr.Forster mentions as being still retained in the Greek church also. Their numbers, however, in Malabar, have greatly decreased, the greater part of the Nestorians and Christians of St.Thomas who settled there

having joined the Catholic church in 1599; this union having been (as before mentioned) brought about by the Portuguese Prelate, Alexis Menezes, the first Archbishop of Goa. Upon the subject of their origin, Fra Paolino adduces the following reasons in support of his opinion that they come from Persia or Chaldea: 1st. Because the Arabs established in India are also foreigners; 2nd. Because the Jews there were originally from Persia; 3rd. Because the Christians of St.Thomas, as well as those of the same sect in Persia, follow the Syrio-Chaldaic ritual; 4th. Because their bishops formerly were ordained in Persia; 5th. Because the Christians of St.Thomas in India, like those of Persia, were in the earliest periods Nestorians; and, 6th. Because, on an accurate examination, a great similarity is observed in the worship and religious practice of both. He afterwards adds a fact that appears to the translator more corroborative of his opinion, almost, than any of the above reasons, viz. that they called God "Allaha", the Holy Ghost "Ruha", etc. These evidently are Arabic. Now had they been originally Indians, as he observes, why should they not have used Sanskrit words? It is certain that in old Arabic authors frequent and familiar mention is made of the Nestorians, as a sect well known in Arabia and Persia.

2. The Sheikh had omitted the circumstance of the destruction of the fortifications, by the Portuguese.

3. The catastrophe that according to Maffeius, followed their evacuation of the fort at Calicut, is not even alluded to by the author.

4. That Albuquerque, Capralis and Almeida were in some respects "buccaneers" their own histories clearly prove.

5. The translator has been unable to find elsewhere any mention of this shipwreck; Maffeius mentions the treaty entered into by the Portuguese, with the Ray of Tanoor, but describes the occasion of it in quite a different manner.

6. Upon this original discomfiture (which however probably amounted to no more than the loss of a few small vessels) Maffeius is altogether silent. That the Sheikh's account of the catastrophe is on the whole true, may be presumed from the

accuracy that it must have been seen he usually displays in his detail of events.

7.   This is an expression of resignation used by the followers of the Prophet in all their distresses. In the Alf Leilah (or Arabian Nights) it occurs at least a hundred times.

Section V

Relating the building of the fort at Shaleeat by the Franks,
and the accommodation again brought about
between them and the Zamorin.

This event happened in the following manner: one of the
principal men[1] of the Franks, setting out from Cochin by land, and
concealing his designs under the false and treacherous pretence of
peace, presented himself before the Zamorin. Now this person was
master of the greatest subtlety and cunning, and capable of
employing the deepest stratagems. He was acquainted, moreover,
with certain of the chief Mahomedans (of Malabar) who were
engaged in trade, and had transacted business with them at the time
when the armistice between the Zamorin and the Franks permitted
such intercourse. And proceeding on to Funan, from thence he went
to the Ray of Tanoor, with whom he remained in consultation until
he had effected a reconciliation between him and the Zamorin. Now
the Zamorin, who captured the fort of the French at Calicut, was
weak and possessed of but a limited understanding and of few
mental resources; being, moreover, addicted to habits of inebriety.
But his brother, who during his reign resided at the ports, and who
succeeded to the government of the Zamorin after his death, was
one who commanded respect, being a man possessed of great
courage and resolution, and not one who considered himself tied
down to the observance of forms, however ancient their institution.[2] By means of these qualities, he obtained the Rayship of Tanoor
before he became the Zamorin, and succeeded to the sovereignty
(of Calicut), which, with all its dependencies, he bequeathed with
an undisputed authority to his successor. But it was during the reign
of this prince that the Franks erected their fort at Shaleeat, in the

vicinity of which the Zamorin, his troops, and indeed all travellers of whatever description, were obliged to pass; it thus commanded the trade between Arabia and Shaleeat, since between the last city and Shaleeat the distance was scarcely two parasangs.[3] The Zamorin had given them permission to build this piece of fortification, after his accommodation with the Ray of Shaleeat; and in consequence of this permission, the Franks setting sail in a large vessel laden with all the necessary materials and instruments for building this fort, arrived in the Shaleeat river at the end of Rubi-al-Akhir, in the year 938 (A.D.1531). Here they constructed fortifications of great solidity and strength; and throwing down the ancient Jamie mosque, which had been erected there on the first introduction of Islam in Malabar (and of which, with the more modern mosques, mention has been made in the preceding pages, they took the stones which had composed this building as material for their fort, to which they also added a church. But whilst engaged in the building of this fort, one of the Franks having carried away a stone of the Jamie mosque above alluded to, the Mahomedans of Shaleeat complained to the viceroy of that nation, who in consequence proceeded thither with some of his officers, and gave orders that stones and quicklime should be supplied by the latter for the work; promising the Mahomedans, at the same time, that no materials but such as were the property of the Franks should be taken for building these fortifications. On this the Mahomedans being satisfied, went away, feeling indeed thankful; but the day after this only, the Franks coming again in a vast concourse, proceeded entirely to destroy the Jamie mosque, so that not one stone remained upon another. Beholding this, the Mahomedans renewed their remonstrances to the viceroy; but this person, in reply to their complaint, answered them, that the Ray of the town to which they belonged had sold to the Franks both the mosque and the ground on which it stood. On hearing this they returned much dejected; for after this they were compelled to assemble for prayer in a small mosque, situated at a great distance from their dwellings. In addition to all this, these wicked men demolished the tombs of the Moslems, and carried off the stones of which they had been built to complete their fortress. Before it was finished however, the Zamorin died, when his brother (of whom some account has been given before) succeeded him; and he, putting an end to the armistice, commenced hostilities against the Ray of Shaleeat, and laid waste his territory; so that at length he was compelled to submit to the Zamorin, and to implore such terms from him as that chieftain was disposed to dictate. And in this year the emir Mustapha of Room, arrived from Mahurrah, at Diu, off Guzerat, bringing with him some cannon and much valuable property. And the prince Toghun, the son of king Ayass, was at this time exercising the government at Diu, as the representative of sultan Bahadur Shah. Shortly after the arrival of the emir at Diu, the Franks made their appearance before it, entertaining a design of seizing upon that place; but the emir engaged them, drove them back, and repulsed their attack with great vigour;[4] the Franks by the permission of God experiencing on this occasion a signal defeat, were entirely broken, and compelled to sheer off much shattered and disheartened.

Notes:

1. Either Alphonso Albuquerque, or his son Francisco, must be here alluded to, as these two persons appear to have conducted the greater part of the negotiations entered into between the Portuguese and the Zamorin about this time.

2. The reason for this digression of the Sheikh's is not very evident, unless, in the comparison which he here draws between the two Zamorins, he means to express his amazement at the oversight (unaccountable in this prince from his great capacity) of the latter of these chiefs, in allowing the Portuguese to establish themselves in so formidable a position at Shaleeat, which was only two leagues distance from Calicut.

3. The word in the Arabic is 'fursukhein': a fursukh is about 18,000 feet, or about three and a half English miles. Their motives in the construction of this fort were here correctly enough judged of.

4. This was the unsuccessful expedition of the Praetor Nonnius, when, by the gallantry of the Turk Mustapha, he was completely

defeated. Maffeius describes the chagrin and rage of the Praetor at this unexpected repulse. ---. This, the third, attempt against Diu, was made, according to Souza, in consequence of positive orders having been sent from Europe that it should be obtained possession of on any terms. The Portuguese fleet rendezvoused in Bombay harbour (in 1531), preparatory to sailing to attack Diu. The expedition, according to the accounts of the last quoted historian, consisted of one hundred sail of vessels of all descriptions, including, transports, these contaning 3,600 Europeans, 2000 natives and Malabars, and 8000 Caffre soldiers, besides 500 Indian boatmen, in all 22,300 men. Having besieged and taken Beli and captured there sixty pieces of cannon, the fleet sailed out to Diu, where they met with a desperate resistance, from the Muslims, under Mustapha Khan Rumi, a European Turk, which repulse induced the main body to return to Goa; whilst a part of the fleet, under Anthony de Saldana, revenged themselves for their disappointment in failing against Diu, by burning Muzaffurbad lying between Beli and Diu.

Section VI

Concerning the third treaty that was entered into between the
Zamorin and the Franks.

This accommodation took place in the year 940 (A.D.1533):
the Zamorin making peace with the Franks upon the condition of
permission being given him to navigate every year four vessels from
Calicut to the ports of Arabia. And this being arranged, certain of
his vessels at once set sail for the Arabian main, his subjects also
generally recommenced trading to different countries, carrying the
passes of the Franks. And after this pacific adjustment the Zamorin
sallied forth to attack the Ray of Tanoor, continuing to war against
and pursuing him, until he purchased peace by surrendering to the
Zamorin the lands contiguous to Funan, and the island in the
neighbourhood of Shaleeat,[1] the Franks who had come from
Cochin, for the purpose of building the port at Shaleeat, acting as
mediators between them in this pacification. Shortly after this, peace
being made between these chieftains, Khoajeh Hossein Sanjakdar,
the Turk and Kunju-Alee-Murkar the brother-in-law of Ahmud-
Murkar, arrived in certain grabs, bringing with them the vast presents for the sultan Bahadur Shah[2] to the Zamorin besides much
money: the sultan being desirous of enjoying the Zamorin's influence, towards inducing the Mahomedans of Malabar to proceed
to Guzerat, to cooperate with that monarch in a maritime warfare
against the Franks. But the mission of these persons was unsuccessful. Now the date of their arrival at Calicut was the 16th of
Rubi-al-awal, in the year 941 (A.D.1534).

Notes:

1. The Ray of Tanoor early evinced towards the Portuguese a friendly disposition: hence the hostility of the Zamorin. He eventually became a convert to the Catholic religion, having been baptized at Goa.

2. The prince was slain in an affray with the Portuguese (according to Maffeius), an account of his death shortly following.

Section VII

Regarding the peace made between
Sultan Bahadur Shah and the Franks: and the grant of
that monarch to them of certain ports.

Now in the latter part of this year, sultan Humaioon Badshah,[1] the son of Babur-Badshah[2] (may both rest in peace!) after having conquered Delhi and the country around it, turned his step towards Guzerat, laying waste that country and driving before him Bahadur Shah; who, in consequence, dreading the loss of his dominions from the attacks of that monarch, sent messengers to the Franks begging their assistance. Thereupon, they consenting to afford it to him, and having to his succour with all expedition, a treaty of alliance and amity was entered into between them; he, the sultan, making over to them certain ports, as a consideration for their alliance, viz. Wusee, Muhaeem, and others.

And the Franks setting up their rule in these parts, and adding to them other towns and lands in their neighbourhood, in this manner made a great acquisition of territory; their power increasing so much that Diu submitted to them, and their authority in this quarter became undisputed; half of the imposts of tenths were also assigned to them. And they exercised their government over Diu, adding to the fortifications of that port also. Now it should be observed that the Franks had, for a longtime before this, eagerly desired the possession of this port,[3] having appeared before it several times with the view of attempting its seizure; first in the time of king Ayass, and afterwards in the time of his children. But they had failed in their designs on all these occasions, having by the divine permission been frustrated. But now that with this their desire, the will of Almighty God accorded, their acquisition of that port was not a difficult task. Moreover, the Lord omnipotent (whose name be praised!) decreed, that the sultan Bahadur Shah should meet his death at their hands; for so it happened, he having been killed by them, and his body swallowed up in the sea.[4] To God and towards him alone, do I look in hope: For the fiat of God, which is irreversible, had gone forth. Now this monarch was slain on the 3rd of Ramzan, in the year 943 (A.D.1536). And after Sultan Bahadur Shah had thus been added to the number of martyrs, these Franks conquered the whole of Diu, settled there; such being the decree of the All-gracious, the All-wise; for against the will of God there is no avail, nor can His resolves be diverted. Now in the year 944 (A.D.1537) the Franks made a descent on Puranoor, killing in this attack Kuttee Ibrahim Murkar, the nephew of Alee Ibrahim Murkar, besides others, at the same time: and after having committed great devastation they returned, being guilty of this wanton attack notwithstanding that they were at peace with the Ray of Tanoor and his people, who with the inhabitants of Puranoor were sailing from port to port, unprepared for such usage; the occasion of it appeared was, that a vessel had sailed to the port of Jeddah, laden with pepper and ginger, without the pass of the Franks having been taken out, who, to prevent a repetition, had recourse to the above-mentioned act of violence; as by permitting this trade in pepper and ginger (which indeed they had made contraband) to be carried on without the restriction of their passes, they necessarily would become great losers, and especially if such were carried on to any large extent with the port of Jeddah. In consequence, however, of what they had done, the Zamorin set out for Cranganore, to attack them and their ally the Ray of Cochin. But after allowing some days to be lost, God infused into the heart of this chieftain a dread of these people, under the influence of which he returned from thence panic-struck, without having effected anything. Encouraged by this, the Franks built a fort at Cranganore,[5] by which and other acts of theirs, the Zamorin was reduced to the last extremity. And about this time Alee-Ibrahim Murkar, and his brother-in-law Ahmud-Murkar, and his brother Kunjee-Ali-Murkar, sailed out with twenty-two grabs in the direction of Kaeel, and arriving off Bentalah, they landed, leaving their grabs at anchor there, themselves remaining on shore for some days. But destruction overtook them on the arrival of the Franks, who came upon them in their galliots, attacking and capturing all their grabs; thus, by the decree of God and his will, many Mahomedans on this occasion suffered martyrdom. Now this capture of the Franks took place in the latter part of the month of Shaban, in the year 944 (A.D.1537). And those of the party above-mentioned who escaped, set out from Bantalah for Malabar; but when they had arrived at Nillaneez, about half of the distance which they had to accomplish, Alee-Ibrahim-Murkar, surrenders his soul to God, to whose mercy, boundless in extent, be it committed. Furthermore, in the middle of the month of Shawal in this year, the Franks (upon whom may god ever send destruction!) seized certain grabs belonging to the people of Calicut, whilst in sight of Cannanore.[6]

Notes:

1. D'Herbelot, upon the authority of Mirkhond and Khondemir, thus traces this Sultan's descent: - "Humayun, son of Babor or Babur, son of Omar Sheikh, son of Abu Said, son of Miran Shah, son of Timur or Tamerlane." He succeeded his father Babur, A.D.1530. This prince ascended the throne of Delhi (the first time) in the year 1530. After a reign of troubles he was compelled in 1542 to flee for safety to Persia. Nine years after this he was restored to his kingdom. His death, according to Ferishta, was melancholy. He had been walking on the terrace of the royal library in Delhi, and while descending the stairs to go below, the stick which he had in his hand, and on which he was resting, slipped, and the king in consequence was projected forwards. When taken up he was insensible, and about four days after (Ferishta tells us) his spirits took its flight to paradise. Humayun died in the year 1556, aged fifty-one, after reigning at different intervals for twenty five years.

2. This prince was son of Omar Sheikh Mirza, and was the first of the house of Timour, after Timour himself, that reigned over Delhi. He ascended the throne in 1475, and died in 1530.

3.   The Portuguese, as the Sheikh here states, appear to have greatly coveted the possession of this island, having, as must have been already seen, directed every attempt to be made for its capture. Its importance fell with the power of the Portuguese, it having then dwindled into insignificance.

4.   The Sheikh is guilty of a great want of candour on this occasion, in suppressing the particulars of Bahadur Shah's death. This prince had unsuccessfully attempted the assassination of Nonnius, or Nuna de Cunha, the Portuguese praetor; and in the affray that followed the discovery of this piece of treachery, to avoid falling into the hands of the Portuguese (who were on the point of taking him), he leapt into the sea, where his death, according to Maffeius, was rather the result of accident than design; when sinking, he called out for help, which was about to be afforded to him; --- Faria-y-Sousa's account of the matter entirely agrees with one given by Maffeius; it seems, however, that there was intention of treachery on both sides. The author of the Mirat Iskundary's account differ but little from Ferishta's.

5.   This fort was built by the Portuguese in 1505, and according to Fra Paolina, taken by the Dutch in 1663. They subsequently sold it to the Rajah of Travancore, from whom it was taken by M.Lally, in command of Tippoo's army, in 1790.

6.   These were some of the captures of Almeida and Cabral, two commanders whose naval exploits are detailed in all Portuguese accounts of their early government in India.

Section VIII

Of the arrival of Soliman Pasha at Diu,
and its neighbourhood

And in the above-mentioned year (A.D.1537) Soliman
Pasha,[1] the vizier of the sultan Soliman-Shah (of whom mention
has already been made), with a vast naval armament, in all amounting
to one hundred sail of grabs, palaccas, and of vessels of a similar
description, appeared before Aden, and attacking it, slew Sheikh-
Aamen-Ebn-Daood the Sultan,[2] with a great many of his principal
nobles, making capture also of the city? After this he proceeded to
Guzerat, and commenced hostilities against Diu; and when, from
the vast calibre and weight of the ordnance with which he had been
furnished by the master (the sultan Soliman Shah), most of the
fortification of that place had been destroyed, and were not in a
condition to admit of further resistance, God created in the heart of
Soliman-Pasha a panic,[3] and infused into his mind a violent dread
of the Franks, under the influence of which, he returned without
having made any impression upon them, first to Egypt, and afterwards to Room. And in thus decreeing it, the Almighty (whose
name be praised!) designed to make trial of the faith of his
servants. After the Pasha's departure, the Franks set about repairing the breaches that he had made in the walls of the fort; and these
being completed, they exercised their rule over Diu in undisputed
sovereignty. Now a year after the death of Alee-Ibrahim-Murkar,
his brother-in-law Ahmud-Murkar, and his brother Kunjee-Alee-
Murkar set sail with a fleet of eleven grabs for Ceylon; but the
Franks overtaking and furiously attacking them, succeeded in
capturing all their grabs, after many Moslems had received martyrdom. But those that escaped, with the men of substance above-

mentioned, made their way to the Ray of Ceylon, who inhumanly put them all to death, having treacherously attacked them. To God, and towards him only, do I look in hope!

Notes:

1. There were two Suleymans, but this is the « Solimanus Peloponnesius » of Maffeius.

2. Having obtained permission to land some of his men, for the recovery of their health as he feigned, he hereby availed himself of the unsuspecting kindness of the Sultan to introduce some of his soldiers into the fort; and these having inhumanly put the prince to death, obtained possession of the place. Maffeius mention this act with terms of just execration.

3. This was the celebrated defence of Diu by the Portuguese in the year 1538, against the combined forces of Soliman Aga, the Turkish admiral, and Khoejah Zaffur, the former having commanded the fleet, and the latter the land forces.--- On hearing of Diu being attacked, Nuno de Cunha (praetor Nonnius), who was the viceroy at this time, sent a fleet of one hundred and sixty sail, which according to Faria-y-Sousa carried one thousand pieces of cannon, and five hundred men, to reinforce the garrison.

Section IX

Of the fourth treaty entered into between the
Zamorin and the Franks.

Now the Franks coming to the Zamorin, who was at this time in Funan and praying for peace, he consented to make terms with them; the Rays of Tanoor and Cranganore, who are also at Funan, were instrumental in bringing about this pacification, which took place in the month of Shaban, in the year 946 (A.D.1539). And after this adjustment of differences, the subjects of the Zamorin resuming their commercial occupations, again traded under the protection of passes from the Franks. And on the eighth day of the month of Mohurrum (the sacred), in the year 952 (A.D.1545), the Franks put to death a Mahomedan of great consequence and consideration named Aboobukur-Alee, who was residing at Cannanore, involving also in his fate his near relative Kunjee Safee.[1] Now the first of these was uncle to Alee-Azraja, and the second, his father; and in consequence of their being put to death hostilities again broke out, but shortly after the matter was accommodated.

Notes:

1. Respecting the cause of this act of hostility on the part of the Portuguese the Sheikh is silent, nor has the translator been able to find in the history of Maffeius any mention of these persons. They probably fell in some of the petty rencontres between the Portuguese and their countrymen, which their mutual animosity made frequent.

Section X

Of the recurrence of hostilities between the
Zamorin and the Franks.

The occasion of this rupture was as follows:

On the first day of Mohurrum, in the year 957 (A.D.1550),
a league had been entered into by the Zamorin with one of the
chieftains of Malabar, who was the most powerful of all the allies
of the Ray of Cochin, his territories beings contiguous to Cochin
on the southern side; and this chief the Franks had named "the lord
of the pepper lands," (or "the great pepper-owner,") in consequence of the large quantity of that spice that he usually collected
from the different districts where he grew.[1] And he became one of
the adherents of the Zamorin, who confirmed to him the possession of his Government. He made a petition also to the Zamorin,
that he would make his brother fourth in the line of succession, as
he himself would succeed as Zamorin after the death of that chieftain, and upon the demise of his two brothers after him: - in compliance with which request, the Zamorin made him fourth in the line
of succession, according to the custom which had existed from old
times among the people of Malabar. And shortly after this, this
great pepper lord being on his return to his own country, the Ray
of Cochin, with the Franks, marched out to intercept him; and
attacking him, they followed up their hostilties until they had
accomplished the death of this chieftain, he having been destroyed
by fire: this happened in the month of Jumadee-al-awal of this year.
And when the intelligence of his death reached the Zamorin, he set
out with all expedition from Calicut, to take revenge upon the
authors of it; and reaching the territories of the (late) lord of the
pepper lands, he commenced hostilities against the Franks and

their ally, the Ray of Cochin, expending in this warfare such good substance, which never returned either to himself or to his posterity. And on the 8th of Jumadee the second, of the above year, a large body of the troops of the deceased chief appeared before Cochin, having the river flowing between them and that town; and proceeding to attack it, they burnt a vast number of houses of which it was composed, and occasioned great loss to its inhabitants, being provoked to this assault in consequence of their chieftain having been slain in the expedition of the Ray of Cochin and the Franks (whom may God Confound) against his territories. From all these causes, then arose that hostility, which now raged at its highest, between the Zamorin and the Franks[2]; and the latter at this time sailing out from Goa, after warlike preparations of great magnitude, made a descent upon Turkoy, burning and destroying the greater part of the houses and shops of that town, and also the Jamie mosque that was there. And this was on the morning of the Sabbath,[3] on the 14th of the month of Shawal, in the year before-named; and five days after, in the early dawn, they made a descent upon Fundreeah, burning the chief part of its houses, and also four Jamie mosques of great size that had been built there. And on these occasions, in each of these towns, a third of the inhabitants received martyrdom. Now in the month of Jumadee the second, in the year 960 (A.D.1552), news arrived of the death of the chieftain alee, of Room, who had fallen a martyr when fighting against Franks (whom may God visit with that destruction which befell Aad and Thamood).[4] To God, and towards Him only, do I look in hope! Such being the decree of Him who is all-gracious and all-wise! Before the death of this chieftain, however, he had seized upon certain ships belonging to the Franks, and had made a descent upon Pun-Kaeel, a village in the neighbourhood of Kaeel, where some Franks were dwelling, whom he attacked and destroyed, laying waste the place itself also. Furthermore, in the month of Rujub, in the year 960 (A.D.1552), Yoosuf, the Turk, sailed from Diu-Mahal to Funan, against the monsoon, carrying with him cannon of a large calibre, and of great weight of metal, which he had taken from the Franks who were dwelling in Diu.

Notes:

1. This probably was some chieftain whose territories lay in the neighbourhood of Aleppi and Quilon, where the greatest quantity of pepper was formerly grown and exported.

2. Maffeius relates in his history, numerous descents of this nature made by his countrymen on the territories of the Zamorin. As he commonly, however, omits to mention the date of these several expeditions, it is not easy to say to which of them the above account alludes to.

3. The Jewish Sabbath, or Saturday.

4. These were two ancient Arabian tribes to whom they say the Prophet Salih was sent; but having rejected him, they were overtaken by destruction.

Section XI

Regarding the fifth armistice that was agreed upon
between the Zamorin and the Franks.

In consequence of the determined inveteracy manifested by
the Franks, and from the increase of poverty and decay amongst
the Mahomedans, the Zamorin was induced once more to consent
to terms with them; after this his subjects again traded under their
passes as the commercial communities of other states then did: and
this pacification took place on the first day of Mohurrum, in the
year 963 (A.D.1555). And about two years (or a little more)
afterwards, a quarrel took place between the Franks and the
Mahomedans residing at Cannanore and Durmuftun, and in the
districts in the neighbourhood of these places, which continued for
nearly two years: hostilities being mutually carried on between them;
after which time the matter was settled, by the Mahomedans
submitting to the imposition of the commercial passes, established
by the Franks, as they had done in former times. And during this
warfare against the infidel Franks, Alee-Azraja, a Mahomedan
leader of great consideration (upon whom may God shower down
his best blessings!) greatly distinguished himself, having exerted himself with superior zeal and bravery, and lavished his wealth without
sparing in the cause; although he was not seconded in these his
efforts by the Ray of Koltree, or by the great body of the population of his dominions. In consequence of the zeal shown by him,
however, these cursed Franks (whom may God abandon to
destruction!) set sail in a fleet of galliots to attack the islands of
Malabar,[1] which belonged to Azraja, and which acknowledged his
authority; and arriving amongst them, they made a descent upon
the island of Ameni,[2] slew a vast number of its inhabitants, and

made captives of more than four hundred souls, men and women. They plundered also everything of value that it contained, and burnt the greater part of the mosques and houses that were upon this island. And before their descent upon Ameni they had visited Shatelakum, where they had put to death the chief part of its inhabitants, and taken many prisoners. Now the natives of these islands are the whole of them an inoffensive race, being possessed neither of arms, nor any means of defence whatever. Notwithstanding this, a large portion of them suffered the death, being victims to the barbarity of the Franks. And amongst these was a man of great virtue and piety, one who was far gone in years, and also a woman, who was his equal in goodness and piety; for although these were possessed of no means of self-defence, yet the Franks seized them, and put them to death in the most cruel manner, casting earth and stones upon them, and striking them with blows that caused ghastly wounds, persevering until death released their victims from their barbarity. May God, whose mercy is unbounded, have compassion on their souls! To return, however, these islands are many in number; but the principal ones, and those which contain cities are only five; and these are Ameni, and Kordab, and Anderoo and Kaluftee, and Mulkee; and of the smaller ones, the most inhabited are Accance, Kunjumunjula, and Shatclakum. But God be praised who is most high! For when he would make trial of His servants, He caused the Franks to prosper; establishing them in the greater part of the sea-ports of this part of the world. For instance, the ports of Malabar, and of Guzerat, and the Concan, besides others which He gave into their possession, permitting the influence of their rulers to extend over numerous countries; for in these later days they have built fortresses at Hurmoz, Muscat, Die-Mahal, Shumtura, Milaeed, and in the Moluccas; and at Meelapoor and Nagapatam, and other parts of Solmandel also in many harbours of Ceylon. Furthermore, they have found their way to the Chinese empire, carrying on trade in all the intermediate and other ports, in all of which the commercial interests of the Mahomedans have been in consequence consigned to ruin; the traders of that religion having been at the mercy of the Franks, and, of necessity, subservient to them; the faithful, indeed, having been prevented from carrying on any trade but that for which they have neither turn nor inclination, whilst the traffic that was most congenial to their pursuits, and afforded the largest return, was interdicted to them, as the Franks have rendered it impossible that any others should compete with them in it. Now the first blow that they inflicted upon the trade of the Mahomedans, was their making contraband their traffic in the articles of pepper and ginger; afterwards, they were excluded from the trade in the bark of spice trees and in the clove jilli-flower, and the herb fennel, and in the produce of this kind, the returns and profit of which were very considerable. Lastly, they were cut off from having any commercial intercourse with the Arabian ports, and with Malacca, and Resha, and Thinasuree, and other places, so that there remained to the Mahomedans of Malabar, of their coast trade, nothing but the petty traffic in Indian-nut, coconut, and cloth; whilst their foreign voyages of trade were confined to the ports of Guzerat, the Concan, Solmandel, and the countries around Kaeel. It should be understood further, that the Franks, in building some of these forts, designed to prevent the people of Malabar dwelling about Honnore, Basilore, and Munjilore, from collecting rice in granaries, and exporting it, as was their custom from these places to Malabar generally, to Goa, and even to the Arabian ports. But the Franks (Heaven confound them!) extorting the produce from the cultivators of the lands, and extending themselves over all quarters of the world, have vastly increased in number; having also brought under allegiance to them the governors of the different ports, so that their authority at last has become undisputed. Moreover, they have cut off all maritime trade, except that engaged in under the protection of their passes, and with the admission of their sovereignty of the sea: their own trade thus becoming daily more extensive, and the number of their ships constantly increasing, whilst the interests of the Mussalmans have every day become more depressed. Notwithstanding all this, however, no reprisals have been made, either of their ships or forts, if we except that made by that holy warrior Sultan-Alee-Alshee (upon whom may God shower down his blessings!) when he took from them Shumturah, and made it a rallying place for Islam (for which act may God distinguish him by a reward adequate to its merit!); also the captures by the

Zamorin, who surprised the forts of the Franks at Calicut and Shaleeat; and that of the Ray of Ceylon, who captured, at different times, all the forts that the Franks had built in that island, but which, however, was eventually conquered by them, like other places. Now the Franks, up to this period, had abstained from molesting those who were in alliance with them, and who carried their passes, committing no injury against the masters of the vessels, who had not the protection of those passports to show, except, indeed, for some special reason. From this year, however, they delivered their passes to the masters of the vessels on their proceeding to sea, and if they were lost, by the vessels being wrecked by storm, or from any other disaster, they would seize the ship and its cargo, putting to death all the Mahomedans and others on board of it; and this in the most cruel manner, cutting their throats and throwing them into the sea; binding them with ropes and tying them up in nets, or in some other ligatures of the kind, and then casting them overboard. Further in the year 970, or a little before it, they seized, in Goa, upon a large body of Mahomedan merchants who were collected there, endeavoured to force them to embrace Christianity, and continued to torment them until the greater part of them outwardly became converts: but, after a time, they made their escape out of their hands, flying with whatever portion of their property, they could recover, and again returned to Islam, thus glorifying God and their religion. But an Abyssinian woman, who refused to become a proselyte, they persecuted to such a degree that she died.

Notes:

1.   The Laccadive Islands.

2.   Ameni is one of the largest of the Laccadive Islands, which were discovered by Vasco de Gama in 1499. Their poverty usually protected them from invaders, as they produce no grain, but merely coconuts, plaintains, and betel; they are at present subject to the Beebee or princess of Cannanore. It is remarkable that Maffeius throughout his history never alludes even to their existence: from this it seems probable that the expedition against them (above alluded to) was undertaken by private individuals, rather than by order of the king of Portugal, or his representative the viceroy of Goa.

Section XII

Of the occasion of hostilities being again renewed between the Zamorin and the Franks, and of the sailing out of the former with a fleet of grabs to attack them.

Now in consequence of the increase of acts such as those detailed above, on the part of these Franks, and from the decay of condition evident amongst the Mahomedans, produced by the depression of their commerce, which was now entirely cut off, parties of the inhabitants of Baduftun, Turkoz, Fundreeah, and other towns, having equipped certain small grabs, and armed themselves with weapons for defence, sailed out to sea, carrying with them no passes from the Franks, but being resolved upon resistance, and prepared for it. And they seized a great number of grabs and vessels belonging to the people of Kabkad, and the new port, and Calicut, and Funan; these all being subjects of the Zamorin. They captured also, besides these, a great number of ships and grabs belonging to different nations, taking a great many prisoners, by which means these adventurers possessed themselves of great wealth. For God willed that the star of victory and success should now rest upon them, instead of that cloud of uniform ill-success which had hitherto overshadowed them in their wars, chiefly owing to the fierce inveteracy of the Franks exerted against them. They made capture, moreover, of a considerable number of ships belonging to the Pagans of Guzerat, the Concan and other ports; and, in consequence of these seizures the maritime trade of the Franks becoming greatly curtailed (as they could make no voyages now except with and sailing in fleets), and finding their profits in consequence diminished in proportion, they commenced an indiscriminate plunder of the property of the Mahomedans, being guilty of great oppression and tyranny, and particularly in the following instances. As the chief port of those who were the owners of the grabs were persons without the power of resistance, and possessed of but little property, and as the greater number of these vessels belonged to several and joint owners, upon the defalcation of any customs due upon the property of any of the Pagans (who shared in the ownership) they would seize upon the vessel, and upon all that it contained, although part of it should be the property of a Mahomedan: in this manner they possessed themselves of the full amount that had been expended by the latter, notwithstanding that it had been stipulated at the time of the vessel's being entered for the voyage, that the property of the Mahomedans should not (in the event of such partial defalcation) be touched. But when they once had confiscated any property, they would never make any restitution of it to its owner, for there was no one amongst them who could compel them to this act of justice; whilst the Ray of the town usually divided with them what they had thus iniquitously obtained. Nor was it any avail to protest against this treatment, the Franks being a contumacious and insolent race, and but few of them entertaining any fear of God! And about the middle of the month of Ramazan, in the year 974 (A.D.1566), the inhabitants of Funan and Fundreeah, accompanied by others, having sailed out from the former of those ports in a fleet of twelve grabs, captured a carracca belonging to the Frank which had arrived from Bengal, and which was laden with rice and sugar, being at the time of its capture in sight of Funan. Furthermore, on the Sabbath, on the eighth day of Jumadee the second in the year 976 (A.D.1568), another party of the same people, and from the same port, sailed out in a fleet of seventeen grabs (amongst this grab being Kutti Poker), and made capture of Shaleeat of a large carracca, which had sailed from Cochin, having on board nearly a thousand Franks, many of them approved veterans; the vessel also being fully equipped in every respect, and containing much precious merchandize. But whilst they were engaging the carracca she took fire and was burnt;[1] not however before the Mahomedans had saved some of her largest guns. And there fell in this action more than one hundred of their fighting men, and persons of rank, besides servants and inferiors: whilst those who escaped the sword perished in other ways, some being drowned and others falling victims to the flames. Now praised by God for all this! And sometime after this success, these townsmen sailing out in the direction of Kaeel, took twenty-two vessels belonging to the Franks and their allies, which were laden with rice, which they had partly seized upon in Kaeel and in its neighbourhood, and partly had brought from Coromandel and other parts. And besides the rice on board of these vessels there were three small elephants, which they carried into Funan, and disembarked in the river there. And in the latter part of Jumadee the second, in the year 978 (A.D. 1569), the individual named Kutee-Poker before-mentioned, having sailed at night into the river which runs near Munjiloor, with six grabs, succeeded in firing the greater part of the fortifications belonging to the Franks there; taking also a small galliot of theirs; and he made good his passage without the loss of a single vessel. But when within the sight of Cannanore, he fell in with a fleet of nearly fifty galliots belonging to the Franks, and engaging them, he received martyrdom (surely the unbounded mercy of God has embraced him!). neither did anything that was in his company escape, not even a single grab. Now this was a man of approved zeal and determined courage in this holy warfare against the Franks (whom may God confound!). Shortly afterwards, that great warrior Alee Azraja, the chief of Cannanore (upon whom may God shower down all blessings!); beholding the inveteracy and persecution, which was bringing ruin and the last poverty upon the Mahomedans by putting an entire stop to their commerce, and that all this proceeded from these cursed Franks, despatched an envoy to that great sultan and most beneficent monarch Alee-Aadil-Shah (whom may God ever defend and prosper!), complaining to him of what the Mahomedans of Malabar were suffering from the oppression and tyrannical treatment of the Franks, and begging his aid for their delivery from the evils that affected them; calling upon him also in the name of the All-merciful, to take up arms against these infidels. Further to promote his suit also, he sent presents to that monarch; whose heart God most high having awakened, he prepared an expedition against the fort at Goa, which was now the seat of the government of the Franks, but which had formerly been subject to Jeddah, that city of high dignity. It should be observed moreover, that a treaty had been entered into between Aadil-Shah and Nizam Shah (upon both of whom may God shower down his blessings!) after the capture and destruction of Beejanuggur and the death of its Ray; wherein they agreed to attack with their combined forces both Goa and Sheiool. And after the despatches of Azraja had reached Aadil-Shah, he, with his court and army, set out and halted above Goa beginning to harass the Franks, and to intercept their supplies.[2] At this time also, Aadil-Shah sent a messenger to the Zamorin with his royal credentials, informing him of his having commenced his attack upon Goa, and calling upon him for his cooperation, in prohibiting all provisions from being carried from his dominions to that place. Now the Zamorin and his subjects, as has been shown, had been carrying on hostilities against the Franks for many years, when this envoy of Aadil-Shah arrived; the former being indeed at that very time at Shaleeat, employed in concerting plans to attack them. Further Nizam Shah[3] with his troops and followers at this time proceeded against Sheiool,[4] the fortifications of which place he had begun to batter with cannon of heavy metal; and the capture of that place would have been very practicable had it not been for some delay, and the distrust which was entertained by Nizam Shah towards Aadil Shah. This failure also, in part, arose from that chief's having overrated the power of the Franks, all which induced him to raise the siege, and to make peace with them.[5] In this unsuccessful attempt Aadil-Shah should be exempted from all blame; for Goa was at a long distance from the troops who were besieging Sheiool, whilst the river running between them prevented his joining them. Moreover the former fortress was an elevated one, and its defences were very extensive, so that no power could have prevailed against it unless it had been assisted by succour from on High. Besides this also, the ministers of Aadil-Shah tampered with the Franks, designing to surrender him up to them, and to bestow the sovereignty of Bijapoor upon one of his relations,[6] who was with them in Goa. But that monarch made a timely discovery of the conspiracy; and alive to his danger, he privately withdrew himself from his troops; and when he had reached a place of security, he sent for them (his ministers), having got them into his power, he brought them to punishment, degrading them from their dignities. Further, Aadil-Shah at this time made a truce with the Franks, chiefly in consequence of certain urgent causes that made it necessary for him to do so,[7] and which the Franks discovering, hastened to fortify Goa with lofty and extensive defences, so that no entrance in that place could be practicable, unless God, all-merciful and all-wise, should ordain it otherwise. It should not be forgotten also that Aadil-Shah was as well the victim of treachery as Nizam Shah; the ministers of both having been bought over by the Franks (those enemies of the faith!) and having conveyed to them supplies, and generally succoured them. May God reward them with a retribution commensurate to their deeds!

Notes:

1. Faria-y-Sousa mentions that the ship of Don Joan de Castro (the son of the famous viceroy of that name) was attacked by two Malabar praws, and whilst engaging them, blew up. This however was some years after, and therefore could not be the ship here alluded to by the Sheikh, of which capture no mention is to be found in any Portuguese historians.

2. Ferishta erroneously states A.D.1568 as the year in which Aadil Shah made this attempt to recover Goa, the Portuguese accounts which made it a year later, agreeing with our author. He descended the Poonda Ghaut, his force, according to Faria-y-Sousa, amounting to 100,000 foot, 35,000 horse, 2140 elephants and 350 pieces of cannon; whilst the Portuguese had only, to oppose them, 1600 men and thirty pieces of cannon.

3. Murtuza Nizam Shah who according to Ferishta was commonly called "the Mad." He was put to death by his son, under circumstances of great cruelty, A.D.1586.

4. This is the "Choul" as it is now called.

5. This is the unsuccessful attempt of Murtuza Nizam Shah against Revadunda, a Portuguese settlement near Choul, mentioned by

Ferishta as having taken place in this year. That historian describes the failure of Nizam Shah to the treachery of some of his officers, who were bribed by presents by the Portuguese (chiefly of wine he tells us) to permit the passage into the fort of some provisions. According to Faria-y-Sousa, the force of Nizam Shah amounted to 8000 horse and 20,000 foot. During the unsuccessful assault of that chief, 200 Portuguese deserted from the fort over him.

6. Ferishta made no mention of, nor even alludes to, this intended piece of treachery, merely stating that Aadil-Shah was obliged to retire after having suffered a great loss and effected nothing; nor has the translator been able to find any admission of it in the history of Maffeius. Faria-y-Sousa however confirms the Shiekh's account, informing us that Louis de Ataide made overtures to Noor Khan (a Bijapur general) to assassinate Ali Adil Shah, on promise of his being supported by the Portuguese in ascending the throne. The treachery however was discovered and prevented; Ali Adil Shah raised the siege after being ten months engaged in it and losing 12,000 men, what by the sallies and the exposure of his army.

7. Most probably the desire which possessed him at this time of attempting the capture of Adoni, a hill fortress of great strength, and which, after a long and close siege, was ultimately taken by his general Ankoos Khan.

Section XIII

Relating the siege of the fort of Shaleeat, and its capture

The Zamorin having now in some measure recruited his resources, resolved on making an attempt upon the fort of Shaleeat,[1] being urged to this by the harassing attacks against him persisted in by the Franks, whilst the Mahomedans also were instrumental in exciting him to this act of retaliation. From their exhortations to it, indeed at the time of the expedition against Goa, he had been chiefly induced to undertake it; and since that time, had only waited for an opportunity, it not being then practicable for the Mahomedans to despatch to him the vessels and grabs, which were necessary for the execution of his design. He now, however, sent against this fortress certain of his ministers in command over the Mahomedan inhabitants of Funan, who were assisted by bodies of the people of the town of Shaleeat, and who, during their advance, persuaded the people of Pumoor, Tanoor and Purpoorangar to join them. The Mahomedans entering Shaleeat on the night of the 14th or 15th day of the month of Sufur, in the year 979 (A.D.1571), a battle took place between them and the Franks, at the break of the following day, during which the Mahomedans burnt the houses belonging to the Franks that were without the fort, and their churches also, demolishing at the same time their outer works of mud. Of the Mahomedans three only found martyrdom in this affair, whilst a large body of the Franks were slain, who, after this, retreated to their citadel of stones, and took refuge in it; but the Mahomedans, with the Nair troops of Zamorin, surrounded it (whilst the faithful from all the countries around hastened to engage in this holy warfare), and throwing up trenches around it, blockaded it with the greatest vigilance, so that no provisions could reach the besieged excepting by chance. In carrying on this siege, the Zamorin expended a vast sum of money about two months after its commencement, he himself came from Funan, to conduct it; and with such extreme vigour and activity did he pursue his measures, intercepting all supplies, that the stock of provisions of the Franks became entirely exhausted, and they were compelled to devour dogs, and to feed on animals of a similar vile impure nature.[2] In consequence of this scarcity, there came out of the fort, every day, large bodies of their servants and proselytes, both male and female, who were not molested by the besiegers, but had a safe passage granted to them. Now, although the Franks sent supplies to their countrymen shut up in Shaleeat from Cochin and Cannanore, yet these never reached them, their convoys having been attacked and destroyed. During the blockade, the besieged sent messages to the Zamorin, offering to capitulate and deliver upto him certain large pieces of cannon which were in the Fort, and also to indemnify him for the expenses of the war, besides some other concessions. But he refused to consent to these terms, although his ministers were satisfied with them. Shortly after, when the Franks perceived their condition desperate, from the failure of this provisions, and that they could make no easier terms, they sent messengers to the Zamorin, offering to deliver up the Fort, with its arsenal and all its cannon, provided that a safe passage was afforded them, and protection for their prosperty guaranteed; and he consenting to these terms, the garrison marched out at midnight on the 10th of Jumadee-Alakhur, safe egress being afforded them; they shortly afterwards were sent away (greatly dispirited) with the Ray of Tanoor, who had leagued with and abetted them, being, indeed, secretely favourable to this cause, although ostensibly supporting the Zamorin; and this chief having provided them with all necessaries, conducted them to the Tanoor country, whence galliots sent from Cochin conveyed them to that city, where they arrived in safety, but much disheartened and cast down. Now all that here befell them was in retribution for their evil deeds. Shortly after, the Zamorin having taken possession of the ordnance and stores contained in their fort, demolished it entirely, leaving not one stone upon another. And he made the site where it had stood a barren waste, transporting to Calicut the greater part of the stones and masonry of which the fortifications had been composed, whilst he gave the remaining portion of it to be appropriated to the rebuilding of the ancient Jamie mosque, which the Franks had demolished for material to build their fort; and the ground on which the fort had stood and that lay around it, the Zamorin awarded to the Ray of Shaleeat, according to a stimulation which had been agreed upon at the beginning of the war. Not long after the capture of this fort, and when the Zamorin had already possessed himself of its ordnance and stores, a relief for the garrison arrived from Goa, on board of some galliots and other vessels; but discovering what had happened, they returned in great haste, much astonished and grieved. This, by the permission of the God most High, and through his gracious aid. For in all that here happened, was the mercy and gracious favour of the Lord towards us and all Mahomedans clearly manifested!

Notes:

1.   The Portuguese fort or factory is called Jalleat by Ferishta, whilst Maffeius styles it "Ciales" and Faria-y-Sousa "Chale." That Maffeius should give no account of its capture is extraordinary. --- Faria-y-Sousa states the force of the Zamorin on ths occasion at 100,000 men. Had not Ataide (the viceroy) been at this moment superseded by Norone, the fate of Chale, that writer thinks, would have been different.

2.   The Zamorin proposed terms to Ataide at this time, but that brave commander answered him that he would make no peace, but upon such terms as the Zamorin might expect, were the Portuguese in the most flourishing condition. He had succeeded in concluding a highly honourable peace with Nizam Shah shortly before this period.

Section XIV

Regarding the affairs of the Franks after the capture of their Fort of Shaleeat

Know, then, that these accursed Franks, in consequence of the capture of their Fort at Shaleeat, entertained tenfold rage and hatred towards the Zamorin and the Mahomedans, looking eagerly for an opportunity to carry desolation into the territories of the former, and to rebuild their fortifications at Funan and Shaleeat, so that they might again be enabled to harass and annoy the Zamorin and his Mahomedan allies, in retaliation for their having taken their fort at the latter place.[1] But up to the close of the year 987 (A.D.1579)(by the divine permission) they had attempted in vain the accomplishment of their designs; having in this interval, however, made a descent upon Shaleeat, and burnt some of the houses and shops of that place, which happened on the 22nd of the month of Shawal, in the year 980 (A.D.1572): and in the year following, they landed at Purpoorangar, on which occasion four Mahomedans suffered martyrdom, whilst a large number of the Franks were slain. From these attacks on their part, it appeared very evident that these people had no inclination to make peace with the Zamorin; and particularly after the capture of their fortress of Shaleeat, that event having irritated them beyond measure, both against that chief and the Mahomedans, and caused them eagerly to desire the destruction of both. Subsequently, in the year 985 (A.D.1577), they made a seizure of nearly fifty grabs of different sizes, belonging to the Mahomedans, which at the time of their capture were upon their return voyage from Tulnad, where they had been to load with rice. Now, many of those who were on board these vessels received martyrdom; indeed, of Mahomedans and of the crews of the vessels, nearly 3000 men were slain, whilst the track of the former by their blow became almost annihilated; a calamity which was permitted to visit them, out of the inscrutable designs of the All-gracious and All-wise, of which we can obtain no knowledge, save that a glorious award shall wait those who have fallen fighting for God, and who have practised purity and forbearance. Further, we have hopes that the Lord (whose name be praised!) will bestow upon these everlasting happiness, and comfort them by granting them His heavenly consolation. Verily, God most High has said, "After torment comes care."[2] "For every evil has its good and every suffering its benefit." And in the early part of the year above mentioned, the Franks (may God confound them!) seized upon a large number of grabs belonging to Guzerat, that were proceeding from the port of Surat to the fortified harbour of Jeddah, at the time of their capture being on their return voyage. Of these vessels, some belonged to that glorious monarch, Sultan Jelal-ud-deen, son of Akbar Padsha (whom may God defend!), and contained treasure to a great amount; in consequence of which piratical act, hostilities commenced between that Sultan and the Franks.[3] Now, should not these last have restored the property, (confusion to them!) if only for the sake of peace? Nevertheless, we have hope in God (whose name be praised!) that He will vouchsafe his divine aid to the great Sultan Jelal-ud-deen; and that he will succour him with His Almighty power, and favour him in his warfare with this people, and in his endeavours to expel them from his forts of Diu, Guzerat, Doot, Wasee, and from his kingdom generally; for then shall they be expelled from all the maritime towns which they have brought under subjection to them, if the Almighty God, who is omni-potent and all-powerful, shall of His grace so permit it. And shortly after the above related occurrence certain masters of grabs having salied into the river which flows into the harbour of Adilabad, and the Franks having formed a design of possessing themselves of these vessels, entered the harbour and bore down upon them; but perceiving that they could not approach near enough to effect the capture of the grabs above alluded to, they fired the whole of the harbour and burnt the grabs and other vessels that were within their reach, although some of these had with them their passes and covenants, and belonged to Durmuftun and Cannanore, and to other parts. Further, they fired the port of Karaftan; but attempting the same against the port of Dabool, the Naib of that place,[4] (may God protect it!), having by stratagem made prisoners of their chief men and warriors, put to death the greater part of them, and sent off the rest to Aadil-Shah. And about the same time Aadil-Shah (whom may God protect!) despatched certain of his ministers and troops to form a chain of communication round Goa and to prevent the people of the neighbouring provinces from conveying to them any provisions. He despatched also a messenger with letters and presents to Azraja and the Zamorin, and to Kolturee, calling upon them for their assistance in this attack, and blockade against Goa. But when his envoy with his suite and presents had arrived at Koto-Kulam, the Ray of that place seized and imprisoned both him and his followers. Now, this man was the third in the line of succession to the Kolturee, and was the person who would succeed to the sovereignty after the death of that prince, being his immediate heir. And he acted in this way at the instigation of the Franks. But the envoy of Aadil-Shah managing secretely to effect his escape, the Ray before named seized upon all he had with him, with the presents that had been confided to him. Upon hearing which, Azraja and Kolturee despatched letters to him demanding the surrender of this property, but without avail; for had not the bearer of these letters made his escape, he would have been seized, and delivered over to the Franks. This happened in the year 986 (A.D.1578), in which year certain great men of the Franks presented themselves before the Zamorin, for the purpose of treating with him for peace. This chief was at that time at a Pagoda, sacred amongst all the Pagans of Malabar, situated in the neighbourhood of Cranganore, and he consented that the Franks should build a fort at Calicut; but they being desirous to construct it at Funan, the Zamorin would not agree, so that the attempt at an accommodation at this time failed. However, the Zamorin sent back with the Franks who had come from Goa, three of his subjects who were in his confidence, for the purpose of conferring upon the terms of a pacification; and these entering Goa, were met by the Viceroy of that place (who was termed the Bezroo), who received them with extreme courtesy and respect, treating them with all the attention. But after much time had been lost, these commissioners returned to the Zamorin, the conference having been broken off in consequence of the Franks persisting in their demand to build their fortifications at Funan; and this the second unsuccessful attempt at an accommodation took place in the year 987 (A.D.1579); shortly after which, however, a treaty was entered into between Aadil-Shah and the Franks, they paying to him a certain sum of money.[5] But about this time the Ray of Cochin made preparations to attack the Zamorin, in order to expel him from the pagoda above-mentioned; and for this purpose he collected a vast body of men, and sent a messenger to the viceroy of the Franks (the Bezroo), begging his assistance against the Zamorin. Now, this chieftain had but few in numbers, but nevertheless by divine succour he defeated his enemies, repulsing both the Franks and the Ray of Cochin, and slaying a great number of their troops, whilst he with his allies suffered but little, notwithstanding the disadvantage of their number. Exasperated by this defeat, the galliots of the Franks sailed out from Cochin for the purpose of harassing the trade of the Mahomedans; and they soon captured a great number of their vessels and grabs (may God confound them!), possessing themselves also of booty to a great value: and in the seasons of the year 990 and 991 (A.D.1582-83) also, they carried on their hostilities with great rancour against the subjects and dependents of the Zamorin; the people of Calicut, of the New Harbour, and of Kabkat, and Fundreeah, and Turkoy, and Funan, making attacks upon them at all times and seasons from the beginning of the year to the end of it; so that the maritime trade of these towns was entirely destroyed, and even intercourse between neighbouring ports completely cut off. Moreover, the importation of rice from Tulnad was greatly hindered, so that a great famine, such as never before had taken place, was the consequence, the common people of the ports above-mentioned being deprived of all means of subsistence; and although they had done nothing to call down such a visitation, the Franks continued to seize upon their vessels and grabs,[6] until their miseries were at their height (may God drive out from amongst us this tyrannical race, and save us from them!). However, towards the end of the season of the latter year, a treaty was entered between the Zamorin and the Franks, whereby the latter were permitted to build their fort at Funan; which accommodation was followed by a general exchange of prisoners, the Mahomedans delivering over to the rulers of the Franks their captives of that nation, and the Franks delivering over to the Zamorin those of his subjects that they had taken, and also receiving from that chieftain the prisoners that he had made. Further, the Franks delivered up to the Zamorin the Mahomedan captures that they had made, but these last were few; and there was an agreement entered into between the Franks and the Zamorin regarding the building of the fort before mentioned, which was to be commenced when the viceroy of that nation should come to visit the Zamorin in the following year. In the first season after this, four ships arrived from Europe, on board one of which was the new viceroy of the Franks, who had been appointed by their emperor.[7] Of these vessels, two anchored at Goa, whilst two remained at anchor off Quilon; and the chief of the Franks who had before exercised the government was at this time deposed.[8] Now, no interview took place at this time between the Zamorin and the new viceroy (who had lately arrived from Europe), as the latter did not present himself to the Zamorin, having, without making any story at Calicut,[9] proceeded on to Goa; although the Zamorin had prepared a great many precious rarities, which he had designed as presents to the Viceroy, when they should meet, but his trouble was thrown away. However, when intelligence of that person's arrival at Goa reached the Zamorin, he despatched certain of his principal men to him, when a treaty and league of amity was entered into between them;

the Zamorin obtaining for his subjects permission to trade to the ports of Guzerat and to other parts as in former days, with the privilege also to the port of Calicut to open a trade with Arabia at the end of each season. May God prosper the affairs of the Muslims, and repair their losses, and ever guard their destinies from evil!

Amen! I say, Amen!

The End

Notes:

1. About this time it was that Sebastian (who had ascended the throne of Portugal) divided his eastern empire into three governments independent of each other. The consequence was a train of perplexities that distracted the Portuguese more than all the previous attacks of their enemies in India.

2. Koran, Soorah 94th chapter, which consists only of four or five verses, in which Mahomed, according to Al-Beidavi, alludes to the cleansing from the black drop of sin which he received from the hands of Gabriel in his youth.

3. This is the Sheikh's account of the matter; but that of the Portuguese historians appears a more probable one.

4. This person, according to Ferishta was Khoajeh-Alee-Sheerazee-Zamorin.

5. The terms of the peace were simply an alliance offensive and defensive (if the Portuguese historian may be credited), without any payment or cession of territory on either side.

6. It was usual at this time for fleets to be annually sent out to cruise off the Malabar Coast, on the pretence of suppressing piracy, but which were themselves occupied solely in piratical attacks. Not many years after, a "bull of Croisade" was sent out from Europe, which directed the Portuguese to reduce the infidels by force of arms and the faith, as in other words, to make no scruple of plundering pagodas and sacking mosques.

7. This was Don Francis Mascarena.

8. Ferdinand Tellez de Menezes. The reign of this viceroy was very short, he having been appointed only six months before the arrival of Mascarena, who was the first viceroy, appointed by Philip, and selected by him in consequence of his former brave defence of Choul against Nizam-Shah.

9. Mascarena was commissioned to proclaim Philip in India; and as he found the Portuguese settlements in great confusion owing to the distraction of party, it is probable that the uncourtly treatment that the Sheikh here complains of was in some measure unavoidable.

Index

Books by J.B.P More

1) **The Political Evolution of Muslims in Tamilnadu and Madras,** 1930-1947, Hyderabad, 1997

2) **Freedom Movement in French India, The Mahe Revolt of 1948,** Tellicherry, 2001

3) **L'Inde face à Bharati, le Poète rebelle,** Tellicherry, 2003

4) **Muslim identity, Print Culture and the Dravidian factor in India in Tamilnadu,** Delhi, 2004

5) **Bagavadam ou Bhagavata Purana, Ouvrage Philosophique et Religieux Indien**(edited by JBP.More with Introduction and Index, Preface by Pierre Filliozat, Telicherry, 2004

6) **Puthucheriyil Bharatiyar** (in Tamil), Pondicherry, 2003

7) **La civilisation indienne et les fables hindoues du Pantchatantra** (edited by JBP.More with Introduction), Nirmalagiri, 2004

8) **Religion and Society in South India: Hindus, Muslims and Christians,** Nirmalagiri, 2006 (Preface by Professor Francis Robinson of London University)

9) **Tamizhaga Muslimkalin Parinama Valarchi** (Tamil), Tiruchi, 2006

10) **The Telugus of Yanam and Masulipatnam : From French rule to Integration With India,** Pondicherry, 2007

11) **Partition of India: Players and Partners,** Nirmalagiri, 2008

12) **Rise and Fall of the 'Dravidian' Justice party, 1916-1946,** Tellicherry, 2009

13) **Puducheri Valarta Bharathiar** (Tamil) Pondicherry, 2011

14) **Origin and Early History of the Muslims of Kerala, 700-1600, A.D.,** Calicut, 2011

15) **Indian Steamship Ventures 1836-1910. Darmanathan Prouchandy of Pondicherry, First Steam Navigator from South India, 1891-1900,** Pondicherry, 2013

16) **Origin and Early History of the Muslims of Keralam** (Malayalam), Calicut, 2013

17) **From Arikamedu to the Foundation of Modern Pondicherry,** Chennai, 2014

18) **Origin and Foundation of Madras,** Chennai, 2014